Multilingualism and Nation Building

Multilingual Matters

Alsatian Acts of Identity
  LILIANE M. VASSBERG
Attitudes and Language
  COLIN BAKER
Breaking the Boundaries
  EUAN REID and HANS H. REICH (eds)
Citizens of This Country: The Asian British
  MARY STOPES-ROE and RAYMOND COCHRANE
Community Languages: A Handbook
  BARBARA M. HORVATH and PAUL VAUGHAN
Continuing to Think: The British Asian Girl
  BARRIE WADE and PAMELA SOUTER
Education of Chinese Children in Britain and the USA
  LORNITA YUEN-FAN WONG
Key Issues in Bilingualism and Bilingual Education
  COLIN BAKER
Language, Culture and Cognition
  LILLIAM MALAVÉ and GEORGES DUQUETTE (eds)
Language in Education in Africa
  CASMIR M. RUBAGUMYA (ed.)
Language and Ethnicity in Minority Sociolinguistic Perspective
  JOSHUA FISHMAN
Language Planning and Education in Australasia and the South Pacific
  R. B. BALDAUF and A. LUKE (eds)
Linguistic Minorities, Society and Territory
  COLIN H. WILLIAMS (ed.)
Multilingualism in India
  D. P. PATTANAYAK (ed.)
Reversing Language Shift
  JOSHUA A. FISHMAN
Sociolinguistic Perspectives on Bilingual Education
  CHRISTINA BRATT PAULSTON
System in Black Language
  DAVID SUTCLIFFE with JOHN FIGUEROA
The World in a Classroom
  V. EDWARDS and A. REDFERN

Please contact us for the latest book information:
Multilingual Matters Ltd,
Frankfurt Lodge, Clevedon Hall, Victoria Road,
Clevedon, Avon BS21 7SJ, England

MULTILINGUAL MATTERS 91
Series Editor: Derrick Sharp

Multilingualism and Nation Building

Gerda Mansour

MULTILINGUAL MATTERS LTD
Clevedon • Philadelphia • Adelaide

Library of Congress Cataloging in Publication Data

Mansour, Gerda, 1937-
Multilingualism and Nation Building/Gerda Mansour
p. cm.) Multilingual Matters: 91)
Includes bibliographical references and index.
1. Multilingualism–Africa, West. 2. Sociolinguistics–Africa, West.
3. Language policy–Africa, West. I. Title. II. Series.
P115.5.A358M36 1993
306.4′46′096–dc20

British Library Cataloguing in Publication Data

A CIP catalogue record for this book is available from the British Library.

ISBN 1-85359-175-0 (hbk)
ISBN 1-85359-174-2 (pbk)

Multilingual Matters Ltd

UK: Frankfurt Lodge, Clevedon Hall, Victoria Road, Clevedon, Avon BS21 7SJ.
USA: 1900 Frost Road, Suite 101, Bristol, PA 19007, USA.
Australia: P.O. Box 6025, 83 Gilles Street, Adelaide, SA 5000, Australia.

Printed and bound in Great Britain by the Longdunn Press, Bristol.

Contents

Introduction   1

1 Language Diversity in Africa: Myth or Reality?   11
   Defining linguistic diversity   12
   A sociolinguistic assessment of linguistic diversity   16
   Multilingualism and communication   20
   History and environment—two factors conditioning
      language use   21

2 The Spread of the Manding Language and the Emergence of
   Vertical Multilingualism   26
   Manding origins and environment   28
   Long distance trade, state formation and language spread   31
   Language spread in the conquered territories   36
   Socio-cultural identity and language   39

3 Linguistic Fragmentation in the West African Coastal Belt   45
   Environmental impact on social and linguistic
      development   46
   Social organization and language use in autonomous
      village societies   49
   Fragmentation and language shift among small
      stratified societies   51

4 Arrested Development and Regression   56
   The sociolinguistic consequences of the slave trade   56
   The establishment of colonial rule: Divide and conquer   58
   The growth of multilingual urban centres   61
   The sociolinguistic inheritance of the independent
      West African states   64

5 Multilingualism and Social Transition in Contemporary West Africa   73
   A sociolinguistic profile of West African countries   73
   Language policy: Before and after independence   77
   The growing importance of lingua francas   81

Oral communication, education and literacy
in the multilingual context   84

6 The Role of Language in Internal Conflicts   91
Language policy and ethnic conflict in Mauritania   92
Language issues and the Nigerian civil war   94

7 Policy Options: Assimilationist or Pluralist?   100
Language as symbol of social identity and means
of social control   100
The relationship between language and nation   104
Successful assimilation: The case of Arabic   107
The Swiss model of linguistic pluralism   109
Pluralist language policy in the Soviet Union   111

8 Language and Nation Building in Africa   118
Pre-independence liberation movements   118
Independence or transfer of power?   119
Official language—language of national unity?   123
Pluralism and the national language issue   125
Conclusion: The goals of language planning   131

References   136

Index   142

List of Maps and Tables

Map1.   The Manding People and Their Language   27

Map 2. The Mali Empire in 1325   29

Map3.   Trans-Saharan Trade Routes, 10th to 18th Century 32

Map4.   Larger Linguistic Groups in West Africa   69

Table 1. West African Languages Across Borders   67

Table2. Functional Profile of Languages in West Africa   74

Table 3. Languages Used in Government Education   80

Introduction

Over the many years that it took to complete the research for this book I became increasingly aware that a whole dimension was lacking in current studies of multilingualism. Many studies which admirably deal with the formal aspects of communication—*who speaks what language to whom and when*—are unnecessarily limited in scope, because they do not fully take into account the dialectical nature of the relationship between language and society. Even when multilingualism is placed in its social context this is often done in an ahistorical and unsystematic fashion. For instance, the lack of a historical dimension makes it appear as though we were suddenly faced with a totally new problem: *the problem of multilingualism in Third World countries*. This is perceived as a problem because of the assumption, formed unconsciously under the influence of 19th century thought, that there is or should be an organic relationship between language and nation. Accordingly, nations and countries aspiring to nationhood which do not have one national language are considered defective or, at any rate problematic.

One of the aims of this book is therefore to ask some questions not usually asked in sociolinguistics, to de-mystify the phenomenon called multilingualism and to search for its roots. To do this I have found it necessary to go far off the beaten track in order to show how language and language use are inextricably woven into the social fabric. Language and society have to be treated as one whole and that implies that our research into multilingualism should take into account all pertinent aspects of social development and analyse the factors that may have influenced such a development.

As the title indicates, one of the concerns of this book is the phenomenon *multilingualism* which, by necessity evokes its antonym *monolingualism*. Etymologically, the meaning of these two terms is clear: monolingualism is communication through one single language whereas multilingualism is communication through several languages. Yet in the application of these terms a great deal of ambiguity has crept in. Strictly speaking, monolingualism should refer only to those situations where one language is the only means of communication at all levels of social interaction. Since,

1

however, in analysing modern sociolinguistic situations we often deal with larger political units (nations or countries) we would either have to admit that monolingual countries are the exception rather than the rule—due to the failure to assimilate local minorities and large-scale labour migrations—or accept a looser definition. The latter is in fact the practice, for countries such as Britain, France, Spain and Germany pass as monolingual, despite the existence of minority languages and considerable dialect variations.

Further confusion arises from the fact that, linguistically speaking, the borderline between language and dialect is not at all clear. Hence it is possible, for example, for Spanish policy makers to claim, in the name of national unification, that Catalan is a Spanish dialect and for those on the other side of the border to assert that it is a French dialect, whereas the partisans of Catalan consider it to be a separate language.

Presumably a country's claim to being monolingual is based on the fact that the language of the overwhelming majority is the only official language. This being the language of power the others do not count and, at any rate, centuries of assimilationist policies have seen to it that minority language speakers were obliged to learn the official language and that, at least in theory, nobody is excluded from public discourse.

The term multilingualism is equally loosely applied to two different types of situations: countries which have more than two official languages, such as Switzerland, and countries which have considerable internal linguistic diversity with one super-imposed official language. The latter is the most common pattern in Third World countries, including African countries.

As for the ideological baggage that these two expressions carry we only need to compare them to a similar couple—monotheism versus polytheism—to recognise the in-built positive or negative message which we unconsciously receive. Thus monolingualism becomes equated with civilisation whereas multilingualism—according to the biblical story of the tower of Babel—is God's punishment for the wicked. The sociolinguist does not make such value judgements but considers monolingualism and multilingualism to be alternative patterns of communication which may exist at the communal level or at the national level. However, in most cases, it has been the aim of sociolinguistic research to restrict itself to the description of these different patterns of communication. In the light of the current situation in African countries, this does not seem to address the really vital questions.

The questions which present themselves, and which led me into this study are the following: how did the current situation of multilingualism in Africa develop? Is multilingualism really the problem it seems to be, or does this depend on the historical and social context in which it appears? Can it be lived with and if so, how do multilingual societies manage to establish a functioning system of communication? Are there typical stages in the development of human societies which tend to be monolingual or multilingual ? And lastly, assuming that monolingualism is a simpler or more convenient form of social communication, is multilingualism a phenomenon of transition, or are there stable multilingual societies, and what would be their social characteristics?

Questions concerning origins inevitably lead into history, not history of language as it is usually understood, but the history of human social development with emphasis on the role that language played in maintaining particular social formations. More specifically, since the present focus is on the two modes of communication, it is important to discover which social development favours monolingualism and which produces a multilingual situation.

Paleontologists and anthropologists tell us that the earliest human societies were organised on the principle of kinship, with the family as the smallest unit. As human populations grew in size and were able to benefit from cooperation on a larger scale, a number of related families organised themselves into clans. At the end of this line of development stands tribal society, made up of many clans, each made up of many families. In theory at least, the members of a tribe are considered to be descendants of a common ancestor or ancestress. Beside this cultural–mythological bond and the resultant common culture, anthropologists define tribal societies by their adherence to a common language. In other words: one internally uniform language (monolingualism) served all the purposes of communication and group identity in the long line of social development from the earliest human family groupings to the last surviving tribal societies in the remote places of Australia, New Guinea, the Amazon jungle, Africa and Asia until relatively recently. These latter-day tribal societies, however, have long outgrown the stage of single social units maintaining constant and immediate contact which, at the dawn of social evolution is likely to have been the only guarantee of linguistic uniformity.

As social development advanced from the primitive cooperation of hominid family groups to the complex pattern of social rules in a latter-day tribal society, language functions extended and languages acquired an equally complex set of linguistic rules. Part of this elaboration of social and linguistic rules was the development of a set of social devices which limit and control the process of linguistic diversification, devices which only operate under specific socio-economic conditions. In other words, languages can only attain some form of stability if the societies which they serve have attained a certain level of social organisation and economic stability. At the socio-cultural level this expresses itself in the form of a coherent set of beliefs, myths and legends which are transmitted from one generation to the next and in the form of a clearly defined set of mutual rights and obligations which bind the members of a society to one another and to the environment in which they live. Language forms part of this social bond and is at the same time its expression; its fate is inexorably linked to the fate of the social unit to which it belongs.

For the purpose of this study which is mainly concerned with the relation between multilingualism and the social organisation which made it appear, and the apparent alternation between monolingualism and multilingualism, the following six types can be discerned—types which may but need not follow each other in a historical sequence, but which generally correspond to stages in the development of human societies:

Type 1: primitive monolingualism of clan societies;

Type 2: primitive bilingual societies;

Type 3: centrally organised, monolingual tribal societies;

Type 4: multilingual empires;

Type 5: monolingual national state formations;

Type 6: multilingual federations and multi-ethnic newly independent countries.

The above classification is meant to draw attention to the dynamic and dialectical relationship between language and society: each influences and reinforces the other. Because of the vital role that language plays in the living and eternally changing structure of society our model of language use—if it is to be meaningful—has to account for change and relate each major change in social organisation to its corresponding change in the patterns of language use. The correspondence between these types and historical stages of social development has to be understood in a very general sense, since it cannot be said that all societies passed through all these stages, nor did they necessarily follow one upon the other. In fact, they frequently existed side by side in one and the same historical period. One of the reasons for this fluidity is the environmental impact on human societies which may either retard or advance a particular sociolinguistic development.

The following is an attempt at summarising the six types and outlining their main characteristics.

Type I: Primitive Monolingualism

Societies falling into this type have only minimal, small-scale social organisation and have no apparent need for communication beyond the immediate kinship group. Linguistic uniformity is guaranteed through direct and intensive contact within the group, and lack of contact with outsiders speaking other languages. The adjective *primitive* must be understood in the sense of it being the first and purest manifestation of its type. In this sense one can say that the earliest human social units were monolingual, but at the same time—as we shall see in Chapter 3—such types of monolingual communities continue to exist in many isolated parts of Africa, or indeed elsewhere in the world.

Type II: Primitive Bilingual Societies

In this category too there is only minimal social organisation, either at the clan level or at the level of the village. Historically, the first type of societies which are likely to have had a stable bilingual situation are those which brought two different ethnolinguistic groups into more or less permanent contact, without there being any motivation for merging them. Contact situations of this type arose among communities which were more or less forced to co-exist, due to special environmental conditions. For instance, clans of nomadic herdsmen frequently enter into competition, and subsequently into cooperation, with agricultural communities over the use of pasture during the dry season. Yet, because each community has something to offer the other, temporary arrangements may well become permanent ones, and this social division of labour combined with a different mode of life tends to reinforce separate sociolinguistic and cultural identities and create stable bilingual situations. In this they differ from other multilingual situations which have a more transitional character, either because a change in the balance of power makes them break apart again, or because they become integrated and hence monolingual. These types of stable bilingual communities still exist, for instance in the climatic zone immediately bordering the Sahara in Africa. They are likely to have existed ever since the beginning of agriculture created a rift between nomadic clans and settled clans. This rift most probably contributed considerably to linguistic diversification, since in all types of social differentiation language plays an important role in demarcating the limits of group membership.

Type III: Centrally Organised, Monolingual Tribal Societies

These societies are considered more advanced at the level of social organisation, because there is a conscious effort at transcending the narrow kinship bonds and creating a structure for cooperation on a larger scale. Historically, this development took place first among the settled populations and took the form of a loose federation under an elected tribal chief. In some cases elected chieftainship developed into hereditary monarchy, or monarchical rule was imposed by force. In either case the emphasis on the common bond, common ancestry, common ritual, etc. cancelled any tendency towards linguistic variation, and a common uniform language served as an increasingly important tool of social cohesion.

In some parts of the world this stage coincided with the period immediately preceding the entrance into history of a particular people—for instance, the age of heroic epics in Homeric Greece. The kingdoms and chiefdoms of this stage were often idealised in later times as the *Golden Age*, because they seemed to have been inspired by a sense of common descent and common purpose, while still lacking the internal contradictions which developed in later social formations. Although the Homeric Epics were collected and recorded in writing at a later stage, a well developed oral tradition in itself may lead to the establishment of a linguistic model and an elaboration of style, both contributing to the raising of linguistic consciousness. In Africa oral tradition played a very important role and there were many monolingual tribal societies of this kind in the precolonial period. Tribal kingdoms were the last truly homogeneous and monolingual social formations, and in rare cases—if they remained isolated—they managed to make the transition to modern nationhood without incorporating members of other ethnolinguistic groups.

Type IV: Multilingual Empires

Many efforts at transcending tribal organisation produced multilingual social formations in the past. Tribes which grew in size and economic power, having weak neighbours, were tempted to solve their problems by conquest and annexation of territories inhabited by people speaking other languages. This led to the establishment of supra-tribal multilingual empires, some of which enjoyed considerable stability despite their heterogeneity (cf. the Greek and Roman empires). In all of these the language of the conquerors and ruling class tended to become the language of administration and, to the extent that the conquered people came into daily and direct contact with their conquerors, they had to learn the new rulers' language as a second language.

In such multilingual empires there are two possible types of sociolinguistic development: If the socio-economic situation remained stable over centuries and, particularly in cases where the socio- economic and cultural development of the conquered people was considerably lower, bilingualism would increase because learning the conqueror's language proved to be useful. At a later stage the motivation to become fully integrated, linguistically and socially, resulted in whole-scale language shift. As a result the languages of the conquered peoples eventually disappeared and a hybrid, but monolingual society emerged, as it did in most countries conquered by the Arabs in the 7th and 8th centuries. There multilingualism was characteristic for the period of transition only.

In other cases multilingualism or bilingualism developed into a stable pattern, whereby each language had its appropriate domains. Mother tongues were maintained for all private functions, while the conqueror's language was used for all public functions and, typically only the latter was used in writing. This was the case in the medieval empires of Europe which did not result in language shift, and as we shall see, it was also the case in the multilingual African empires of the precolonial era.

Type V: Monolingual National State Formations

Multilingual empires are not the only possibility for transcending tribal organisation and, in fact, many such empires eventually broke up into their various components. Another form of social organisation had its earliest beginnings in loose alliances of related tribes which later became consolidated under powerful monarchies. Some of these became the monolingual cores of the modern European nation-states. However, many centuries passed between the first stirrings of national linguistic consciousness and the emergence of standardised national languages which were deliberately used as a tool for national unification. For example, for many centuries Latin was the language of official records in European countries, among them France. Yet in 1539 the now famous French royal edict (Villers-Cotteret) ruled out the use of Latin for official purposes and prescribed the use of French. However, this and following edicts were likewise aimed at eliminating local variants, particularly Occitan and Catalan. In other words, monolingualism was considered an essential part of nationhood.

The monolingual ideal of a nation played a particularly important role in the formation of new nations in the 19th century, which arose from the collapse of three multilingual empires: the Russian, Austro-Hungarian and Ottoman empires. These new nations invariably based their claim to independent nationhood on linguistic criteria and attempted to make their national borders coincide with linguistic borders. Indeed, up to World War

II the model of linguistically determined nationhood was considered the norm, so much so that the immigrant countries of the American continent, Australia and New Zealand adopted the same policy. Despite the influx of immigrants from all over Europe and the existence of an oppressed original population the only candidates for official languages were those spoken by the founding nations, and all newcomers were expected to give up their languages and assimilate. And thus the rule of the monolingual nation was upheld.

Type VI: Multilingual Federations and Multi-ethnic Newly Independent Countries

In a limited number of cases, the best known one being Switzerland, people speaking different languages decided of their own free will to form a federation which guaranteed equal rights to each group and its language. This became the ideal of some of the national liberation struggles of the 20th century and inspired, among others, the language policy of the Soviet Union. During the two decades after World War II most of the former colonies in Asia and Africa attained independence, which resulted in the creation of a great number of multilingual states. However, their highly diverse ethnolinguistic composition usually required what was thought to be a temporary arrangement: that of adopting the former colonial language as official language of the newly independent state, while planning for status change of the local languages. Meanwhile, European nations are struggling to break the rigid form of nationhood and are attempting to replace it by a new social organisation based on common economic interests.

The patterns of language use in a future united Europe and those of the newly independent states of Asia and Africa are still in the making and, like Type IV, this type of multilingualism coincides with a period of social change: the transition from a closed national or ethno-centric society to new forms of social organisation on a larger scale. In such periods of transition multilingual modes of communication are likely to prevail, however, under certain circumstances, these periods may bear within themselves the seeds of future integration and linguistic convergence. In the multilingual community which brings people of diverse linguistic backgrounds into close daily contact, the rules of social behaviour tend to work in such a way as to reduce divergences, even if this is not the official policy. To study multilingualism means therefore to observe social change at close range and discover the mechanism of language shift or linguistic convergence.

Summary

The above analysis emerged only gradually while this book was being written. Though it played an indispensable role in clarifying my own thought and underlies much of what is presented in the following pages, these pages are deliberately focused on a few questions of a more factual nature, concerning the historical roots of multilingualism in West Africa, its social and environmental context, its present characteristics and future options, as can be seen from the following summary.

Chapter 1 has three purposes: to show why the catalogue of African languages established by linguists is not a reliable source for assessing the degree of linguistic diversity; to propose studies which would show that linguistic behaviour in multilingual countries is governed by social rules (and hence that the fear of chaos associated with the coexistence of many languages is unfounded); and to discuss those environmental conditions in West Africa which appear to be relevant for social and linguistic development.

Chapters 2 and 3 were conceived as illustration of two types of multilingualism: vertical and horizontal; vertical in the sense that several languages occupy the same physical space while forming part of one stratified social organisation, and horizontal in the sense that small autonomous societies live side by side, having little contact with one another. The latter situation contributes to multilingualism when these small societies are incorporated into a modern state structure. To illustrate the emergence of vertical multilingualism in its historical and environmental context I chose the example of the development of Manding society and language spread in the medieval empire of Mali which occupied the Sahel and Savanna region of West Africa. The southern and western limits of this empire, however, coincided with a different climatic zone: that of the dense forests and coastal belt. The societies living in this zone are socially and linguistically fragmented, a development which must be linked not only to historical events but also to the environment.

Chapter 4 is based on the assumption that the conditions described in Chapter 2 would, eventually, have led to the emergence of a socially and linguistically homogeneous state formation. The main focus is therefore on the question why this did not come about, and how trade with Europeans, the conquest and establishment of colonies arrested any such development and created a situation which considerably aggravated the effects of multilingualism.

Chapter 5 is an analysis of the resulting sociolinguistic situation in contemporary West African countries. This reveals that a new dimension has been added to indigenous multilingualism in the form of a superimposed foreign official language and the introduction of western-style education and literacy.

Chapter 6 attempts to deal with the question whether linguistic diversity bears the main responsibility for internal conflict—a spectre which haunts politicians and language planners alike. Two cases are examined in this context: that of Mauretania and Nigeria's civil war.

Given the present state of multilingualism in West Africa (and elsewhere in the world) *Chapter 7* focuses on the two basic options available to a multilingual country: assimilation or pluralism, each requiring specific social conditions and being associated with specific social, political and linguistic consequences. Such options need to be evaluated on the basis of a clear understanding of the twin functions of language in society—to act as a symbol of social identity and, at the same time, to be a means of social control.

Finally, *Chapter 8* examines the language policies of African leaders, the majority of whom have decided to maintain the ex-colonial language as official language. While assimilationist policies usually aim at unification by means of an indigenous language or the language of a substantial immigrant group, these leaders are persuaded that a foreign language is equally suited for that purpose. This chapter therefore aims at coming to terms with the real motives behind such policies and their likely outcome. It further presents the arguments in favour of a pluralist solution and outlines what this might entail, particularly in the light of present political regimes in Africa.

1 Language Diversity in Africa: Myth or Reality?

A great many books, articles and conference papers dealing with African languages and the African language situation state that Africa suffers from an extraordinarily high degree of linguistic diversity. This view was particularly prevalent in the 1960s—the decade when most African countries gained their independence and when the new leaders had to make decisions concerning the adoption of an official language. Chapters 5 and 8 will deal in detail with that subject, but may it suffice to state here that multilingualism and the poor state of linguistic research served as a convenient excuse for maintaining ex-colonial languages as official languages.

While linguistic research into African languages has made great progress in the last three decades, there has been little change in the status of African languages. The purpose of this chapter is thus to shed some light onto the role of African linguistics in the formulation of what might be called the 'multilingualism complex'. The point of view put forward here is that the assessment of linguistic diversity is exaggerated and that one of the reasons for this is the neglect of sociolinguistic studies. The distinction between linguistics (the study of language systems) and sociolinguistics (the study of the social functions of languages) fundamentally affects the outcome of research. The linguist considers all languages to be equal, in the sense that they are all complete and adequate systems to express meaning. African linguists work on the project of establishing a catalogue of languages—each language scientifically described and classified into groups and sub-groups.

Sociolinguists take the society in which these languages serve as a means of communication as the point of departure. Social development in Africa has not proceeded at an equal pace. Consequently the roles that languages may play within a larger social unit, such as the modern state, is bound to be *unequal*. Some languages expand, become lingua francas, while others shrink and possibly die out. Language death is seen as a great tragedy by linguists because a valuable source for studying linguistic structures disappears. The sociolinguist looks upon this with more equanimity—in

11

times of social change this is a normal occurrence. Languages die out when they can no longer serve their community as an adequate tool of social interaction. Another language takes the place of the dying language and grows in size and importance. This is why sociolinguists are concerned with demographic statistics, geographical distribution of ethnolinguistic groups and the social functions that several languages may assume within a given social context. The second sub-section of this chapter thus attempts to outline how sociolinguists go about assessing and analysing multilingualism, while the third sub-section deals with communication patterns in multilingual countries. Finally, in order to set the scene for a closer analysis of sociolinguistic development in West Africa, the final sub-section deals with the question in what way the environment may influence social and, indirectly, linguistic development.

Defining Linguistic Diversity

In order to understand how and on what basis the assessment of high linguistic diversity in Africa was made it is useful to underline a few salient points concerning the development of African linguistics. The first linguists in Africa were European and American missionaries who were sent to a specific colony to found, and later expand, Christian missions. As it was their main goal to bring the Christian message to the African people in whose midst they had settled, it was their first task to learn their language. Furthermore, since the Christian message, particularly in its Protestant form, relies heavily on literacy, it was part of the missionaries' task to analyse the phonology and grammar of the African language in order to devise a writing system, and ultimately, to translate the Bible, the catechism and hymns. This practical goal of their linguistic analysis was always foremost in their minds rather than the development of a scientific methodology.

Nevertheless, their field work became an example and formed the basis for the methodology of linguistic description of unwritten languages all over the world. The first step in this process was to collect data from one particular place, often a village, and possibly only from one or two informants. Alongside with what might be termed 'the body of the language' the researcher also received the native speakers' preconceptions and prejudices concerning their language and its relationship with varieties from neighbouring villages from his informant. Inevitably, and unwittingly, he introduced a problem which is haunting African linguistics until today: the problem of language labels.

The next step—to proceed to other villages, undertake the same work and compare it to his first results and scientifically establish the degree of relationship between a number of local varieties—was rarely accomplished at that stage. In fact, in the context of the actual mission work, it was more likely that in the next valley or across the river another missionary from another country or rival denomination was at work, received a different name for the language he was studying and devised a different writing system, influenced by the rules of orthography of his own language. Thus we are now faced with the phenomenon of having a number of languages entered into the catalogue of African languages where in fact there should be only one.

The following example may serve as an illustration. In a check list of the languages of the Ivory Coast (Ceccaldi, 1974) we find under the entry EOTILE (group AKAN/KWA) that the native speakers call their language 'Mekyibo'; neighbours of the Abure group call it 'Vetere'; Anyi neighbours call it 'Ewutre' and the official appellation used by the colonial administration is 'Eotile'. The language in question was already nearly extinct in 1971 when another researcher counted only about 100 speakers of this language, explaining that this was due to language shift. (As will be discussed later, this is a common phenomenon in economically marginalised areas, such as the southern lagoons of Ivory Coast).

The problem of language labels may be compounded by the fact that literate native speakers cling to the orthography taught at their mission school and reject that of the rival missionary.

This kind of situation was frequently reproduced, even at a time when linguistic research had become independent of missionary work and scientifically more rigorous. No matter how careful a linguist might be in describing his findings as tentative and preliminary, there were always others representing these as facts which were difficult to revise later. A comprehensive method of linguistic description proceeds from step one— the collation of several such bodies of data from different locations and their comparison, *before* an overall analysis is attempted. Only then can it become clear that an observed regular phonological variation marks at most a dialect variation which in no ways impedes inter-comprehension.

Unfortunately the methods of dialectology have only recently been applied in African linguistics, and this for two reasons. One reason seems to be the real Achilles' heel of linguistics, namely that there is no agreement about the defining criteria of what constitutes a language and what is merely dialect variation, neither concerning the types of features which may be allowed to vary within a language (semantic, phonological, morphological, syntactic), nor up to what degree. The European dialectologist works within a previously fixed, though often artificial frame work of a standard language, but is ready to defend the fluidity of his dialect continuum against an over-rigid conception of linguistic borders.[1] In Africa this kind of approach is complicated by the political reality of totally arbitrary borders which, nevertheless, the present regimes are pledged to maintain. Linguistic continuity across borders therefore falls into the category of research which is politically undesirable. But even within a political unit the term *dialect* is frowned upon because of its chauvinist and racist connotations from the colonial period. In order to become acceptable this term needs to be supplemented by the name of the greater linguistic unit of which this dialect forms a part. And this brings us back to square one: in the case of many African language communities the identity of this greater linguistic unit has often yet to be determined, and standard forms which could be accepted by speakers of all varieties have yet to be established.

This introduces another problem area—that of the classification of African languages. Up till now the most common method of classification is the same as that developed in the 19th century with respect to European languages, namely the genetic classification into language families represented by family trees. In Europe some of the parent languages still exist in written records. Even the layman can see that French, Italian, Spanish and Portuguese are languages descended from Latin, and everyone who is in the habit of consulting dictionaries can testify to the great number of cognate words in many European languages, which clearly point to a common origin. The genetic classification of unwritten languages is highly problematic and, consequently, African language trees are constantly being re-arranged and revised. A lot of research concentrates on higher relationships, while the lower relationships are only vaguely defined and, until such time as the opposite could be proved, *there was a tendency to accept and deal with all labels and all known varieties as though they were distinct languages.* The result of this is a tremendously overblown catalogue of African languages.

Apart from the fact that in many parts of the world similarly complex linguistic situations have been discovered, the high proportion of languages in relation to population also needs to be seen in the context of population density. As we shall see, there can be no doubt that sparse population compounds the problem of linguistic diversity.

In the last two to three decades there have been a number of breakthroughs in African linguistics. First of all, a close examination of language lists helped to identify those labels which refer to the same language or dialect (cf. the example of Ceccaldi cited earlier). Other scholars developed new methods of classification, the most comprehensive one resulting in the *Language Map of Africa* (Dalby, 1978) and the *Thesaurus of African Languages*

(Mann & Dalby, 1987)—a method which will be discussed in more detail in Chapter 3. An important aspect of this research is that it is now reaching the layman through contributions to books of general reference, such as *Africa South of the Sahara*. As a result of this linguistic diversity is being put into a more realistic perspective.

While it is not my intention to give a full account of old or new linguistic methods, a similar line of research is worth mentioning in this context, which deals with internal linguistic relationships and, like Dalby's method results in establishing language or dialect clusters. This is based on the *wave theory*—a theory depicting language expansion in the form of waves departing from a monolingual core area.[2] The further a language gets away from that core, the more it comes into contact with other languages which exert an influence on it and start a process of linguistic change which gets consolidated with time. In this way new varieties arise at the periphery of expanding languages. The wave theory has the great advantage in that it relates physical and time distance to linguistic distance in a manner which can be easily visualised. Unlike the formula of language trees it shows that language change is gradual, that linguistic borders are fluid and that the possibility for mutual intelligibility exists for at least parts of the continuum.

In practice this led to surveys which combined linguistic and sociolinguistic methods, as in two of the five country surveys of languages and language use in East Africa.[3] In these cases linguists composed a list of meanings and made a statistical analysis of similar words in related languages and dialects. They presented their findings in the form of charts indicating the percentage of shared vocabulary between pairs of languages. The results of this objective indication of relatedness were then compared with survey data concerning the native speakers' subjective impression of mutual intelligibility. The lack of reciprocity in some of these ratings clearly demonstrate the importance of non-linguistic factors, such as the functional allocation of languages.[4] This has been confirmed by personal observation in Senegal, where speakers of a minority language had less trouble understanding a closely related language which was used in near-by market towns than the native speakers of that lingua franca had understanding the minority language—despite the fact that, objectively speaking, the degree of similarity (shared vocabulary) was the same.

Studies of this kind point to the importance of a multi-disciplinary approach in the assessment of linguistic diversity, an approach which can be called sociolinguistic in the widest sense of that term. As mentioned in the introduction to this chapter, one reason for the exaggeration of linguistic diversity in Africa is the lack of sociolinguistic data. I shall now attempt to outline what type of sociolinguistic and socio-historical research would be necessary to arrive at a more realistic assessment of linguistic diversity at the national level.

A Sociolinguistic Assessment of Linguistic Diversity

If one wants to compare the sociolinguistic situation in several countries it is very useful to establish a formula which is designed to give a quick impression of the type of multilingualism prevailing in a given country. Such a formula should rely essentially on social data: the demographic statistics of native speakers' communities, the internal geographic distribution of languages, information about the use of lingua francas and an assessment of the proportion of the population speaking such languages (either as first or second language). The main emphasis, however, must be on the functional role of the languages coexisting in a multilingual country, so that this formula may become a useful tool in language planning and policy decisions. I should add that I am using the term lingua franca for African languages which have the specific function of serving inter-ethnic communication within a given context. Lingua francas may be, but do not have to be, hybrid languages such as pidgins and creoles. The emphasis is on their function and scope (cf. Heine, 1970).

Sociolinguistic formula [5]

(i) *Majority language*: Into this category I would put a language which either has a native speakers' community of over 50% of the population total; or a language which is widely spoken as a lingua franca at the national level and has the potential of becoming the national official language. Many African countries have no language which would fit into this category, hence (ii).

(ii) *Sub-national lingua francas*: These may be languages with a relatively small proportion of native speakers in relation to the national total, but which nevertheless serve as lingua francas at the district level. Particularly in cases where there is no clear majority language, it is important to indicate such sub-national lingua francas so that the development and public use of these languages may be promoted.

(iii) *Minority languages*: Into this category I would put languages which have either a small native speakers' community (below 10% of the national total); or languages which are used only for in-group communication. In the context of language planning such languages would have the lowest priority in the competition for scarce funds to develop languages for education and other public functions.

(iv) *Special Status languages*: These are all non-native languages, such as the former colonial and present official language which will continue to play a role in education and international communication; or languages used for religious purposes, such as Arabic.

For a more detailed analysis we would need further information concerning the ethnic composition of administrative districts. It goes without saying that there is a considerable difference between a multilingual country made up of almost monolingual districts and one where multilingualism is as prevalent at the district level as it is at the national level. This distinction is important because administrative divisions are the result of internal policy and the respect of ethno-linguistic boundaries facilitates the implementation of such policies as the use of mother tongues in education. On the other hand, linguistic diversity at the lower levels of administration makes such policies almost impossible to implement.

In Guinea, for instance, there is no nation-wide lingua franca and, as elsewhere in former French West Africa, French is the official language. Yet there are a number of homogeneous administrative districts and, at an early stage, the government of Sekou Toure instituted the use of six of its national languages in education.[6] Senegal, on the other hand, does have a nation-wide lingua franca (Wolof, spoken by more than 80% of the population) but none of its large administrative units (*regions administratives*) are monolingual, only two of its smaller units (*departements*) and six counties (*arrondissement*) are virtually monolingual— more than 90% of the population are native speakers of the majority language of that unit.[7] The Senegalese government has been officially subscribing to the policy of mother tongue education since the 1960s, but has not been able to proceed very far with its implementation.

Finally, a sociolinguistic analysis of multilingual situations must differentiate between rural communities and urban conglomerates. In most parts of Africa rural communities have remained largely traditional and monolingual, whereas multilingualism tends to increase with the size and function of towns. Invariably the highest linguistic diversity is found in capital cities and ports. These have to be treated as a separate phenomenon with its own pattern of communication though, frequently, language choice in the urban context tends to reflect a general trend in a country as a whole.

The categories proposed for the sociolinguistic profile are based on demographic data of ethnolinguistic groups on the one hand and the functional role these languages play on the other. If one or more languages in a multilingual country are today expanding as second languages and serve as the preferred lingua franca(s) at the national or sub-national level, this is a vital factor in the assessment of linguistic diversity. It is an aspect which is often neglected in studies of multilingualism and in most cases we have to rely on vague estimates as to how wide-spread a local lingua franca is.

To overcome the predicament of lacking accurate data, the relative position of languages on a hierarchical scale can be assessed by studying the role development of these languages in the historical context of their contact situation. Such an analysis should show that the expansion of certain languages as first and/or second languages, at the expense of other languages, is the result of a long chain of development related to the historical role of a particular ethnolinguistic group, of its socio-economic achievements , or a combination of these and other factors. On the basis of such an analysis the position of dominance of a particular language can be assessed, and relatively accurate predictions concerning future tendencies towards modification of linguistic diversity can be made. The linguistic situation in a multilingual country thus reveals its dynamic aspect and the inherent possibilities for change.

Most studies on multilingualism are handicapped by a totally ahistorical world view and the prejudice that the achievement of national and linguistic unification is a condition for the attainment of nationhood and progress in general. A political scientist (Pool, 1969) wrote in this vein when he attempted to correlate economic development (measured by Gross Domestic Product per capita) with the degree of linguistic diversity, and came to the predictable but false conclusion that linguistic heterogeneity always correlated with a low GDP and that a high GDP correlated with considerable linguistic homogeneity.

The problem with this and similar conclusions is that they do not take into account the source of GDP. If the source is a unique commodity such as oil—as for instance in the case of Kuwait (which on Pool's figure describing the situation in 1962 occupies the top position for GDP)—the correlation of GDP with population or language use is irrelevant. Whether oil wealth is spread over a small, relatively homogenous population or poverty shared by a heterogenous population of hundreds of millions (as for instance in India), in neither case can language use be held responsible.

Attempts at comparing the language statistics of an underpopulated and underdeveloped rural African country with those of European countries are at the same level of muddled thinking. It becomes therefore doubly important to restore the balance, and to deflate the myth of multilingualism by focussing on the historical development and the environmental factors which contributed to this phenomenon.

As outlined in the introduction, the various transformations of human social organisation in general tend to alternate between those organisations which favour monolingualism and those which favour multilingualism. Each phase of socio-historical evolution has its own appropriate pattern of language use. Monolingualism is not necessarily the opposite of multilingualism, rather—one is a variant pattern of the other. For instance, there are many situations where a given geographic space is dissected into small units, each separated from the other by natural barriers and inhabited by a small, isolated community whose language or dialect differs from that of its neighbours. Although in these small communities only one language may be used for all purposes of social communication (monolingualism) their coexistence within a larger social organisation contributes to horizontal multilingualism at the macro level. A variant pattern of multilingualism (vertical) occurs when two or more ethnolinguistic groups share the same territory and participate in joint socio- economic activities.

These two types of multilingualism differ in more than their spatial arrangement (horizontal versus vertical); they differ—most importantly— *in the potentials inherent in each social situation.* While horizontal multilingualism—the patchwork quilt of tiny monolingual societies, living in virtual isolation, is the road to socio-economic stagnation, cultural introspection and marginalisation of the languages spoken by them, vertical multilingualism is usually associated with social change, language shift among the speakers of minority languages and an expansion of one or several dynamic lingua francas. To put it differently, horizontal multilingualism is a dead-end road while vertical multilingualism may lead to eventual linguistic unification.

A particular sub-type of vertical multilingualism is prevalent in the fast growing urban centres in multilingual countries. There the close contact in the daily life of the community—at work, in the neighbourhood, at school and in the market place -contributes to a speeding up of the social process of assimilation and acculturation and, within one or two generations, the population of diverse ethnic origin from the rural hinterland adopts the urban lingua franca as its first language. The urban context is therefore an excellent laboratory for observing the changing patterns of language use.

In any one of the fifteen West African countries [8] the three basic patterns of language use are as follows: monolingualism at the village or district level, stable bilingualism in areas of constant contact and vertical multilingualism in the urban centres. Depending on their sociolinguistic environment, the inhabitants of these countries are to a great extent bilingual or polyglot, and language shift is a frequent phenomenon. Africans seem to be highly motivated to learn more and more languages and are unimpeded by the inhibitions and mental blocks of language learners from monolingual Western countries. The concept that it is a disadvantage to have to learn another language is alien in this context. The only disadvantage which is perceived and relevant is lack of opportunity to learn.

Multilingualism and Communication

To the outsider the process of communication in a multilingual country is a mystery and it is all too often equated with chaos. That this is not the case emerges very clearly from the various investigations of multilingual communities which focus on the functional roles of coexisting languages. There is general agreement among sociolinguists that language choices are determined by the domains of social behaviour (family, neighbourhood, work, etc.) and that we can distinguish between three major functions of communication: in-group communication, out-group communication and specialised communication.

In other words, some languages serve only for communication within ethnic groups and are rarely or never learned by speakers of other languages. In a multilingual context their function may even be reduced to the family. Other languages fulfil the in-group function, but are also used as lingua francas to communicate with members of other ethnic groups. In a multilingual urban context virtually all social activities require the use of such a lingua franca. Specialised communication refers to domains such as religion, education and other public functions in multilingual situations where none of the local mother tongues or lingua francas is considered to be adequate or appropriate.

On the basis of these three types of functions multilingual societies have been classified according to the number of languages needed for full participation in social interaction at all levels.[9] Accordingly, the members of minority groups in European countries, such as the Welsh in Britain, need to master two languages: Welsh for in-group communication and English for out-group communication as well as for specialised communication. Similarly, in countries where the national language is not one of the world's major languages, a certain percentage of the population may have to learn a second language for purposes of higher education, scientific research and international communication in general.

In Africa the most common pattern involves the use of one of the country's mother tongues, a lingua franca and the official language, and is therefore referred to as the *three-language* or *trifocal* pattern of language use.[10] However, under special circumstances, or in highly multilingual countries, a small percentage of the population may be obliged to use two lingua francas—that of the home district and that of the capital—a situation one could classify as a four-language pattern of communication. Although many Africans do in fact learn other languages in addition to those belonging to the above types, their communicative needs as members of a multilingual society can be met with competence in two, three or four languages. This is the important point which emerges from such a classification. Furthermore, it reveals that multilingual communication is rule-governed, socially determined behaviour.

The disadvantages of such communication patterns have been exaggerated by observers used to only one way of acquiring languages: through intensive and prolonged effort in a formal setting. In Africa it is common for children to come into contact with other languages. By the time they reach school age they may have learned two or three local languages at play or in the family. The only language which requires a formal setting— school or rural literacy classes—and which does present learning difficulties is the official language. It is difficult to see how, in the context of poor African countries with dismally low percentages of graduates from Primary, let alone Secondary School, this additional language is supposed to simplify internal communication patterns. To the politically conscious observer it seems obvious that the disadvantages of multilingualism are, on the one hand, related to the social structure of African countries and, on the other, to the language policy of the educated élite. Chapters 5 and 8 will deal more closely with these problems.

History and Environment—Two Factors Conditioning Language Use

If we accept the basic premise that languages share the fate of the societies of which they form a part, it follows that all factors influencing social development also shape languages and the roles they may play. A society which is hampered in its social development because of the hostile environment in which it has to struggle for survival is unlikely to give rise to an expanding language—unless, by its own genius, or because of a particularly fortunate set of circumstances—it is able to overcome the environmental limitations. On the other hand, a society which has an abundance of natural resources can support population growth, and is more likely to develop economically, socially and culturally.

Certain types of environment favour certain types of socio-historical processes which, in their turn foster either monolingualism or multilingualism. For instance, monolingualism at the level of the nation can only flourish in a contiguous geographic space or in a centralised state which deliberately fosters linguistic unity through the imposition of a standard language and by achieving a high degree of literacy. All of these conditions helped to shape and stabilise the language situation in Europe during the last thousand years. Despite the many wars of conquest in both directions and royal marriages which intended to join distant territories, England and France remain separated by the Channel and here the linguistic borders neatly coincide with politico-geographic borders. On the other hand, linguistic unification through the standard languages has *not* resulted in the elimination of all minority languages or dialects. Below the official monolingualism, multilingualism is alive and kicking! What then makes African multilingualism so extraordinary?

The causal link between history, the environment and linguistic development has been recognised by a number of scholars. Alexandre (1967) for instance, points out that in Africa the languages with the widest spread are found in the savanna zones, whereas the greatest linguistic fragmentation is found in mountainous and forest regions, to which one might add the coastal region of West Africa.

In fact, as we shall examine in Chapter 2, early language expansion in Africa took place in the Sahel zone, wedged as it is, between the Sahara and the lightly wooded savanna. In this zone cyclical droughts have had a negative effect on settled agriculture, but rivers and wide open spaces without any physical barriers, made it an ideal corridor for human contact. The existence of two important commodities—salt from the Sahara and gold from the savanna and forest regions—gave rise to a flourishing long distance trade which, in turn, became the basis for state formations. Since the 8th century A.D. several ethnic groups followed one another, dominated the trade routes and founded empires. In each case the language of the ruling group (Soninka, Manding and Songhai) experienced a period of expansion as the favoured lingua franca throughout their dominions. Social contact between different ethnic groups in these multilingual empires led to bilingualism, and even though in many cases the mother tongues continued to be spoken, the wide spread use of the lingua franca greatly facilitated inter-ethnic communication and cooperation.

The reverse situation prevailed in the dense forests, mountains and the swampy coastal belt of West Africa. On the one hand, the environment was more fertile, so that communities could grow all the food they needed. On the other hand, the physical barriers to communication made cooperation beyond the village level difficult, if not impossible, and survival depended on being autonomous. Their continuing physical isolation eventually led to social, economic and cultural stagnation. Most of these small village societies were introspective and hostile to contact, which resulted in the over- emphasis of dialect differences between neighbouring groups and eventual fragmentation of languages.

Only in exceptional cases did the environment of the swampy coastal belt provide possibilities for small communities to exploit the tidal channels as a means of bridging distances and establishing limited trade. In some such cases there was a modest accumulation of wealth which supported greater population growth and resulted in the formation of small, ephemeral statelets (cf. Chapter 3). On the whole, however, this zone is still characterised by a large number of small to tiny language communities.

There is another aspect to the environmental impact. Since a number of West African countries are divided into those two zones: the savanna interior and the tropical forest and coastal belt, this is invariably reflected in a social and sociolinguistic split. For instance, the people of the savanna zone of northern Ivory Coast have more in common with those of eastern Guinea and northern Ghana, in terms of rhythm of life as determined by the seasons and in economic activity as well as cultural–linguistic traits, than they have with their fellow countrymen of the south. The savanna people of Guinea and Ivory Coast use the same lingua franca, while in the coastal areas of these countries other languages assume that function. In fact, most West African countries which use more than one lingua franca share this environmental dichotomy.

Language expansion in the Sahel and savanna, and language fragmentation in the coastal belt—two diametrically opposed processes, conditioned by a different environment and a different social history—are both responsible for the development of multilingualism at the level of the modern African state.

The impact of historical events on sociolinguistic development is of equal importance. In the former Mali empire the evolution from feudalism towards a more tightly organised and more homogeneous state and the development towards nation formation and linguistic unification was prevented by the arrival of the colonial powers. Even the establishment of European trade along the West African coast had a negative impact on such a development, since it was responsible for the final collapse of trans-Saharan trade which had been the *raison d'être* and main support of the African medieval empires. While the empire of Mali crumbled into its smaller ethnic components, European traders directly intervened in the coastal states with alliances, counter alliances and by corrupting the rulers. Rivalry for the material gains offered by European traders led to 300 years of disintegration and chaos. Slave raids and tribal wars heavily decimated some of the lesser organised populations or drove them into the coastal swamps and forest recesses. Others were affected by famines and sought salvation in migration.

During the actual colonial rule of the late 19th and 20th century forced labour, military conscription and labour migrations added to the population movements and created a new type of linguistic heterogeneity: the mixing bowl of modern urban centres and development projects. Onto an already complex system of multilingual language use the colonial rulers imposed their own language and thus prevented the functional development of the local languages. The borders drawn between the different colonial powers were the result of historical accident and thus unrelated to the physical realities of the environment and the traditional, cultural and linguistic units of the population. To these were added further borders—equally arbitrary—to outline the territories of the independent African states.

Every one of these borders cuts across ethno-linguistic units, separating people who belong together and throwing together those who have little or nothing in common. Thus every country has a sizeable list of ethnic minorities, which it shares with one or two of its neighbours, as well as internal divisions which are more or less deeply felt. All this is the heritage of colonialism, a heritage which may turn out to be as fateful as economic dependence, because it made the continued use of European languages necessary, thus adding linguistic-cultural dependence and increased alienation to other heavy burdens.

The question at the head of this chapter—*is linguistic diversity in Africa a myth or reality?*—is one of those questions which has to be answered ambivalently. I hope to have shown in this chapter that there is a great deal of myth involved, on the other hand, the reality of multilingualism cannot be denied. Yet, I would suggest that the natural processes of social interaction are at work everywhere, creating new communication patterns. Furthermore, an understanding of the causes of multilingualism helps to assess the situation in a more rational fashion. With this aim in mind the following chapters focus on a more detailed analysis of the various factors contributing to multilingualism in a number of particular cases.

Notes to Chapter 1

1. This discrepancy between the borders of the standard language, which coincide with political borders, and the actual linguistic continuity of the dialects across the German–Dutch and German–Danish borders is the subject of German dialectology.
2. cf. Bird (1970) with respect to Mande languages, and Djite (1988a) with respect to the classification and labelling of the Kru languages and dialects of the Ivory Coast.
3. cf. Ohannessian & Kashoki (1978) on the languages of Zambia and Ladefoged, Glick & Criper (1972) on Uganda.

4. cf. also the review article by Scotton (1980).
5. I have taken the liberty of borrowing this term from Ferguson (1971), though I disagree with his definition. The relative size of the mother tongue community is, to my mind, less important than the function a language has in a given context; e.g. Swahili has a mother tongue community of only 10% of the Tanzanian population total, but has a long established lingua franca function for at least 90% of the population. Also languages such as English or French can hardly be placed in the same category with the local lingua francas as *major languages* because of their specialised function and restricted domains of use.
6. cf. Mann & Dalby (1987: 187), also Calvet (1987: 176) for its limitations.
7. cf. Mansour (1980).
8. For the purpose of this study West Africa includes the following countries (in alphabetical order): Benin, Burkina Faso, Ivory Coast, Gambia, Ghana, Guinea, Guinea Bissau, Liberia, Mali, Mauritania, Niger, Nigeria, Senegal, Sierra Leone and Togo.
9. cf. Nida & Wonderly's (1971) typology which grades multilingual situations according to the language needs of the individual.
10. cf. Scotton (1982a and b).

2 The Spread of the Manding Language and the Emergence of Vertical Multilingualism

In the previous chapter I referred to the importance of lingua francas in the social communication network of multilingual societies. Whatever the context, lingua franca status not only assures geographic expansion and social prestige of a language, it also tends to attract new native speakers. One of the historically important lingua francas in West Africa is Manding, and this chapter will examine the various factors which contributed to its development.

What makes Manding unique in the West African context is the fact that it is spread over a distance of 1200 kilometres, yet has managed to maintain a relatively high degree of linguistic uniformity. There are native speakers of Manding in nearly all West African countries (cf. Map 1) estimated at somewhere between seven and ten million (to my knowledge, estimates of second language speakers do not exist and would be difficult to assess). In Mali Manding is the undisputed national lingua franca, spoken by more than 80% of the population (either as first or second language) and in many other countries it is an important sub-national lingua franca.

As is the case with many African languages, linguistic research into the Manding language suffers from considerable terminological confusion, thus giving an impression of linguistic diversity where actually there is considerable uniformity. Manding belongs to a group of languages for which linguists have coined the term *Mande* (cf. Houis, 1959; Greenberg, 1963; Bird, 1970; and Whelmers, 1971). This group is subdivided into a number of small, closely related languages and one large dialect cluster for which the native speakers have no all embracing term, although they emphasise their essential cultural and linguistic unity. French scholars have referred to this unit as *Mandingue* or *Malinke* and English scholars as *Mandingo, Mandinka* or *Mandekan*.[1] As some of these terms are also used to

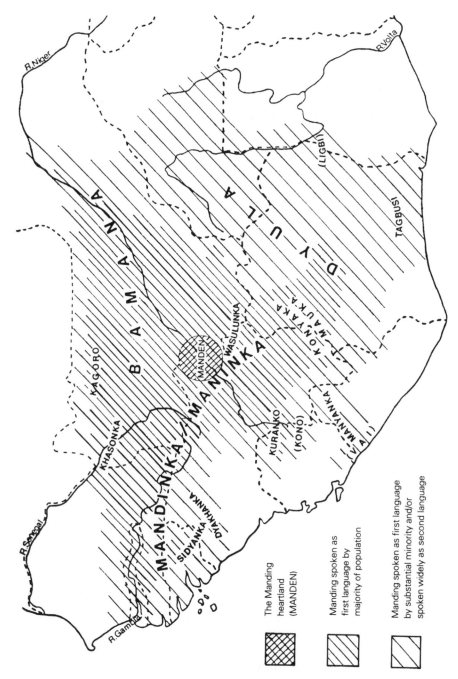

Map 1 The Manding people and their language (from Dalby, 1971)

distinguish specific dialects, Dalby (1971) proposed the use of the term *Manding* to refer both to the people and their language—a practice which I have adopted in this book.

The main linguistic distinction of importance here is that between the central dialects: *Maninka, Mandinka, Bambara* and *Jula*, which share 95% of a common vocabulary and thus retain a high degree of mutual intelligibility, and the fringe dialects which have more non-Manding elements and are less easily comprehensible to Manding speakers.

This high degree of cohesiveness would have been understandable if language expansion had been a recent event. As this contradicts the well documented history of the Manding people, Bird (1970) underlines the importance of extra-linguistic factors, which in this case have led to language stability rather than language change. The factors he mentions are: climate, topology, geographic location, economic activity, social structure and their sense of historical and cultural identity.

Manding Origins and Environment

Historically the Manding dialects are related to the medieval empire of Mali, its trading relations and its military conquests. An analysis of the extra-linguistic factors contributing to the expansion of the Manding dialects and their internal uniformity would therefore have to begin with the original core group, the environmental impact on this group throughout their history, their social structure and economic and political pursuits.

According to oral tradition the cradle of the Manding kingdom—the *Mali, Malel* or *Melli* of the Arab sources—is the province called *Do* (or *Daw*), namely the area around the actual town Segu in Mali (Ly-Tall, 1977; Niane, 1975). From there a severe drought is said to have driven the Manding people further south to the area astride the Niger, between the towns Siguri and Bamako, with the river Sankarani as its eastern limit and the Tinkisso valley to the west (cf. Map 2).

This nucleus kingdom was originally a vassal of the empire of Ghana (not to be confused with modern Ghana), and must have been in existence at the time when the Arab geographer Al-Bakri visited Ghana in 1067, since he relates the conversion of the king of Malel to Islam.[2] The collapse of the empire of Ghana brought the Manding kingdom into the hands of the Sosso (another Mande group) from whom it was delivered by the legendary victory of Sunjata Keita in about 1235 AD. The first expansion phase of the old Manding kingdom took the form of a federation of the principal Manding clans and chiefdoms under the victorious Sunjata. The secondary effect of this victory was to bring a number of non-Manding provinces under Manding suzerainty and, eventually, like its predecessor, Mali

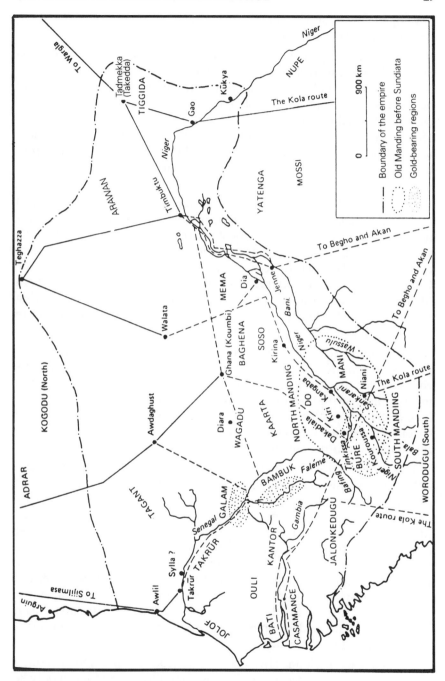

Map 2 The Mali Empire in 1325 (from Niane, 1984)

developed into a supra-ethnic and multilingual empire with far flung provinces and an extensive network of trade.

The old Manding kingdom was situated in the climatic zone called the *Sudanic Savanna*, an area to the south of the Sahel which has a rainy season of three to five months, though in the hot interior evaporation is high and nowadays agriculture is only profitable along river banks. It is possible that climatic and soil conditions have deteriorated here since the days of the Mali empire, for the Arab sources of that period praise the fertility of these regions and the great choice of agricultural products. At any rate, conditions here were better than in the Sahel from which the Manding core group is said to have migrated.

While the major expansion of the Mali empire took place in a westward direction, the Guinean Savanna to the south provided a permanent attraction. With a rainy season of five to seven months, it consists of light forests and fertile land, suitable for the cultivation of rice and home to a number of highly prized forest products such as palm oil, coconut and kolanut. The Guinean Savanna was originally inhabited by people of the Southern Mande group, who traded with Mali and helped to support its growing urban centres. Due to population expansion these Manding cousins were eventually pushed further south into the dense forests.

One feature common to these three climatic zones is the great ease of physical communication, both by land routes and along the numerous rivers, which made this part of West Africa a natural meeting place and ideal for intense trading activities. Trade, whether over short distances or long distances, creates contact between linguistically related groups and encourages contact with other ethnolinguistic groups, thereby laying the foundation for future language expansion.

It is in this sense that environmental conditions, reinforced by socio-economic conditions, can be said to have influenced Manding language expansion. The early development of urban centres and the great mobility of a population, of which only a relatively small proportion was occupied in agriculture, created multilingual contact areas in almost all the later acquired provinces of the Mali empire. The concept of *linguistic geography* has therefore only limited applicability in this part of West Africa and needs to be replaced by the concept of *linguistic stratigraphy*, or vertical multilingualism. Super-imposition of one language on a linguistically diverse population creates the need for bilingualism and opens up the path for greater functional development of the lingua franca, as well as extending its geographical spread.

Language expansion is always the expression of expansion at another level—military, socio-economic, religious or cultural—and it can only be fully appreciated if those other factors are brought into focus. In the historical context of medieval West Africa the control of trans-Saharan trade is likely to have represented the most important opportunity for expansion at all levels.

Long Distance Trade, State Formation and Language Spread

Although there seems to be evidence of trade between the Mediterranean world and sub-Saharan Africa since the 5th century BC, the heyday of trans-Saharan trade began with the Muslim Arab conquest of North Africa in the 7th and 8th century. As elsewhere in the world, trade stimulated urban development and the formation of supra-ethnic states, but its impact depended very much on the size of the political units and their ability to guarantee the safety of travellers. However, the precondition for long distance trade is the existence of a stable set of exchangeable commodities which, in the western zone of trans-Saharan trade, were salt from the Sahara exchanged against gold from the south.

As from the 8th century AD Arab sources mention the trade routes in this zone which were dominated by the empire of Ghana—a Soninka state with its centre in what is now southern Mauritania and northern Mali. There the Saharan caravans converged and the exchange of gold from the area around the upper Senegal river against salt from Sijilmasa and Taghaza took place. Around the beginning of the second millenium, and probably before the north–south axis extended further south, it was complemented by the Niger–Senegal–Gambia axis, also initially controlled by Soninka traders. (cf. Map 3)

Around 1076 the Almoravids (Berbers) conquered Ghana, sacked its capital and undermined the Soninka monopoly. Following this, a struggle for supremacy ensued between the former vassals of Ghana which was eventually resolved in favour of the Manding. It is this event which is celebrated in oral tradition as the glorious victory of the Manding king Sunjata over the oppressor Sumanguru. The Manding proceeded to establish themselves as the new masters of trans-Saharan trade, with its focus on the Manding capital Niani. In the early stage Soninka traders seemed to have continued to ply their routes[3], but later they were either replaced by Manding merchants, or at least by Manding speaking merchants. By the time the Mali empire had reached its zenith it controlled several gold producing provinces and had extended the first north–south trade route along the Upper Niger beyond its sources, to the forests of Sierra Leone from where it obtained a third valued commodity: the kolanut.

Subsequently, around 1400 AD new sources of gold were discovered in the forests of modern Ghana, in the area south of the Volta bend. This

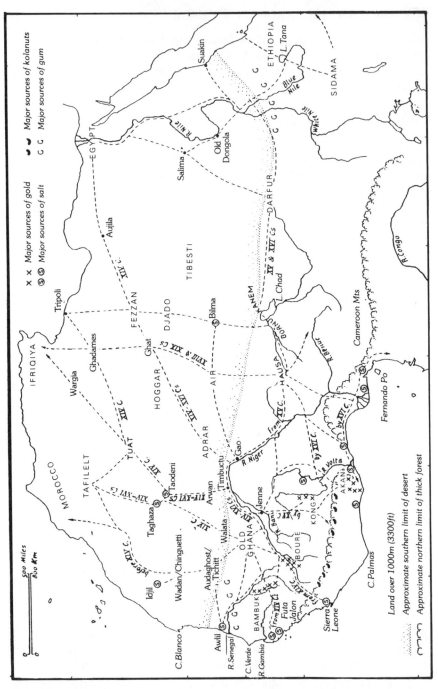

Map 3 Trans-Saharan trade routes, 10th to 18th century (from Fage & Verity, 1978)

became the focus of the third major trade route, which connected the northern towns Timbuktoo and Jenne along several stages with Begho, a town which is thought to have been founded by Manding merchants.[4] Situated in gold producing country, Begho was also centrally located for trade with the Ashanti further south and the Hausa network of trade further east. It was the southernmost Manding settlement, but it seems to have had contacts with the Atlantic coast at Elmina.

After the collapse of the Mali empire (1599 AD) the Manding were no longer in control of the northern Saharan trade routes, but with the arrival of Portuguese traders on the Senegambian coast (1444 AD) and the Gold Coast (1471), the western and southern routes gained in importance and the focus of Manding trade gradually shifted to these routes. Manding influx into Gambia, northern Ivory Coast, Burkina Faso and the West Volta region of Ghana increased in volume, now including warriors as well as traders, and new colonies were founded.

There are three questions of interest to the sociolinguist in this context: Which language was used in connection with the Manding gold trade? How did it spread and how far?

Our first outside information concerning the Mali empire comes from Arab sources, since it was Arab and Berber merchants who formed the northern contacts of this trade. From the 14th century we have three sources: *Al-Umari* (1337), who gives a very detailed account of the empire of Mali, its king, its people and its customs, based on the reports of a 'trustworthy' Arab merchant who lived there for 35 years; *Ibn Battuta* (1353), the well known travelling scholar who visited Mali and recorded many detailed observations; and *Ibn Khaldoun* (1393), the eminent sociologist and historian to whom we owe the genealogy of Manding kings.[5]

The first and much repeated sociolinguistic observation concerns the secrecy with which the gold trade was surrounded. Al-Umari describes the following scene:

> salt is lacking in the interior of the land of the Sudan. There are people who risk themselves and bring it to some of these people who give them in exchange for each heap of salt the like in gold [...] some of the remote people of the Sudan do not show themselves. When the salt merchants come they put the salt down and then withdraw. Then the Sudan put down the gold. When the merchants have taken the gold the Sudan take the salt.[6]

Descriptions of this kind seem to suggest that no language of trade was used, but it is highly unlikely that the people involved in this regular, well organised and economically vital activity were unable to communicate linguistically. Similar exchanges were observed frequently and, indeed, the importance of this method of silent barter seems to lie elsewhere. As recently as 1683 a French traveller[7] described such an exchange where a market official intervened, measuring each heap and collecting tax in the form of a certain percentage of gold and salt. The ban on speech (and hence on direct contact) appears to have been a means of controlling the exchange rate, collecting taxes and generally protecting the interest of the middlemen. But it was not a general practice and was never mentioned in connection with trade of other products.

The other question mark concerns the extent of the use of Arabic, considering that most of the merchants who took salt and other products to the northern cities of Mali were Arabs. Yet despite the frequent comments concerning the high prestige of Arabic scholarship, the use of Arabic was limited to the domain of religion and Islamic law. Ibn Battuta relates how, at every stage of his journey, he was met by a *member of the white community* (an Arab merchant or scholar) with whom he had previously corresponded. Through these he was introduced to local dignitaries, mostly of Manding origin, and in each case he describes how his words were translated into *their language.* In the case of the governor of the northern border town Walata he seems to have been offended by this use of an interpreter (apparently he expected that the governor would address the travellers directly in Arabic). The only persons with whom he was able to communicate directly, even if they were of Manding origin, were the 'qadi of Mali' (chief justice) and the lesser judges, as well as other Islamic scholars who were competent in Arabic. Furthermore, the Arab merchants and scholars residing in the capital of Mali and other towns he visited spoke Manding, and frequently acted as his interpreters.

Later sources concerning language use in trade with Manding merchants are limited to those areas where a Manding trade route made contact with Portuguese vessels. As from 1460 onwards Portuguese sources mention the use of Manding interpreters for trade up the Gambia river and along the Upper Guinea coast. For instance, Hair (1966) cites Cadamosto who recorded that in 1456 he stopped in the Casamance estuary where Manding was the trade language (and possibly the language of administration). On the other hand, he returned from the Rio Geba estuary without having been able to make his intentions understood, which implies that at that time this was the limit of the usefulness of his Manding interpreter.[8] A later witness, Fernandes, wrote in 1510 that the Mandingas were the largest tribe with a single language in Guinea. (In fact the Portuguese were so impressed with the amount of gold the Manding merchants brought them, and the tales of fabulous riches and the might of the emperor of Mali, that the king of Portugal sent three ambassadorial missions to his court.)

The first Portuguese travellers reaching the Gold Coast (Ghana) reported that the title of the local chiefs in the vicinity of Elmina was 'mansa' (the Manding royal title) and some scholars have taken this as an indication of the extent of Manding influence. Fernandes confirmed a few decades later that the gold trade along this route, which reached far north into the interior to Jenne, was in the hands of the 'Ungaros' (one of the names of the Mali empire was 'Wangara'). This label was later replaced by *Jula*, which means 'itinerant trader' in Manding and refers both to the people and the language they spoke and which is still used in that sense for the Manding dialect spoken in Ivory Coast and Burkina Faso.

So much for the spatial aspect of Manding language spread related to trade, as witnessed by historical sources, and it remains to investigate how, in some cases, language spread took place. As Wright's (1977) study of a Manding trading clan in the Gambia shows, these clans had close family ties at every stage of their journey between the Niger and the Gambia estuary. Usually members of this clan had married into local families, obtained land and became trade representatives who were able to provide all the necessary services for passing caravans. The constant coming and going of caravans assured that the link with the home province was never severed and, at the linguistic level, that any tendency towards diversification through local linguistic influence was prevented.

The same pattern applied to the southern route. In both cases Manding settlements had a distinct urban character and—if these were situated among non-Muslim tribes—the Manding merchants (who were Muslims) lived in compact communities around a commercial centre and a mosque. Furthermore, the Manding stock in these settlements was constantly replenished by new arrivals from the Manding heartland or the northern towns Jenne, Timbuktoo and Gao—particularly after these were invaded by the Moroccans at the end of the 16th century. In this way the number of native speakers of Manding in the Gambia, as well as in Burkina Faso and Ivory Coast steadily increased.

Languages also spread through language shift: speakers of other languages at first become bilingual, using the lingua franca side by side with their native language and, eventually, cease to speak that language, so that their children grow up as native speakers of the dominant language. Wherever Manding merchants had trade contacts their language became the lingua franca, and a number of economic and sociocultural reasons encouraged language shift. For instance, the founders of the Niger–Gambia trade axis were Soninka, but later Manding merchants and settlers were in the majority and during the heyday of the Mali empire, the Soninka adopted the Manding language, though their dialect (Jakhanka) still shows traces of their original language. In other cases clan names may be an indication of Soninka origin, even when linguistically speaking these clans are fully assimilated.[9]

In their trading activities the Manding required a great quantity of slaves for porterage which they purchased from local chiefs all along the route. As a consequence these slaves had no common language other than Manding, but through conversion to Islam they could eventually gain their freedom, after which they became fully integrated into Manding society.

Long distance trade was in many ways the most important factor leading to Manding language spread in West Africa, yet to a certain degree trade depended on military power to provide the required safety. The conquest of other territories was also a means of keeping competitors out of the race, and migration to these territories helped to implant the conqueror's language. However, the depth and durability of language spread depended ultimately on how the small tribal kingdom was transformed into a multilingual empire, or rather on how this empire was organised and administered.

Language Spread in the Conquered Territories

As already mentioned above the foundation of the Mali empire is attributed to the Manding king Sunjata whose conquests are celebrated by oral tradition and confirmed by Arab sources (cf. Ibn Khaldoun). At the height of its power (about 1325) the Mali empire extended from the Senegambia in the west to Tadmekka and Gao in the north-east, from the Saharan salt mines (Taghaza) in the north to the forest fringe in Upper Guinea in the south (see Map 2).

The new administrative organisation attributed to Sunjata and his successors distinguishes two categories of provinces in the Mali empire: the traditional Manding heartland and adjacent provinces, and newly conquered 'foreign' provinces. The former appear to have been under direct rule and it is here that Manding language use was consolidated and replaced other languages. The most obvious reason for this was that conquest of the immediately adjacent provinces was followed or indeed preceded by extensive migration of Manding clans, which resulted in assimilation and language shift of the original population. These provinces which form a ring around 'old Manding' originally had a mixed population of Sosso (or Soninka) and Manding, or Jalonka and Manding. The Manding-related clans of these provinces were subjected, confined to the artisan caste and had to pay a special annual tax to the mansa, in particular the Sosso metal workers' clan Kante (the former ruling family) and the Jalonka clans of the Futa Jallon and Tinkisso valley who worked in the gold mines.

All these provinces were governed by the younger branch of the royal family, and this whole area is now homogeneous Manding-speaking territory, with the exception of recently arriving immigrants who speak Manding as a second language. In some cases the dialects of Manding spoken along the periphery of the four central Manding dialects contain traces of one of the contact languages (Soninka or Pulaar) which indicates large-scale language shift in the past and, indeed the speakers of these dialects are still conscious of their mixed ancestry.

Military conquest of the foreign provinces proceeded almost simultaneously in two directions: north and west, and in each case it followed in the footsteps of the Ghana empire and seized its trade routes. However, language spread was affected differently in each case. Most of the northern and north-western provinces, namely the area from the Middle Niger to the Middle Senegal reaching far north into Berber territory in the Sahara, came under indirect rule, and it was particularly in this zone that the waxing and waning of Mali's power was most noticeable.

Rulers of these provinces were invested by the king with their authority and given a Manding title. Only three of these were rewarded for their loyalty to Sunjata with the royal title 'mansa'. Others, such as the main trading centres along the southern edge of the Sahara (Walata, Gao, Timbuktoo and Tadmekka) were ruled by vassals with the Manding title 'farba' (which was translated into Arabic by 'naa'ib', meaning deputy). The various remarks made by Ibn Battuta concerning language use in these towns suggest that some of the officials were of Manding origin, and that it was common to address the people through an interpreter. Among the officials he mentions was the second-most important man after the farba, the 'manshaju', (mansa-joon means king's slave in Manding) a title which he renders in Arabic as 'mushrif', meaning supervisor, whose function it seems to have been to make sure that taxes were paid properly.

From oral tradition we know that Manding culture was and still is very language conscious, consequently it is not surprising to find several references to language use in the Sunjata Epic. In the description of his exile at the courts of Wagadu (Ghana) and Mema it is mentioned that people there spoke Soninka, but that most merchants and members of the royal families also spoke Manding. Once the Mali empire was established Manding became the language of power and influence and during the height of its power all official exchanges were carried out in the Manding language. Even in its diplomatic relations with the king of Morocco and the sultan of Egypt it seems that Manding was used on a regular basis, since Ibn Khaldoun refers to a certain 'al-hajj Yunus, the interpreter for this nation in Cairo'.[10]

However, Manding language spread in the north-eastern parts of the former Mali empire was only temporary, one of the reasons for this being the subsequent historical events. Timbuktoo and Gao, for instance, had been under Manding rule for only one century when these cities were invaded by the Songhai, and their language is still the preferred lingua franca in those towns.

After the establishment of the central and northern provinces the wave of military conquest spread westward across what is now eastern Senegal into the Gambia valley. Essentially this conquest followed the Niger–Gambia trade route which had previously been established by Soninka traders under the protection of the Ghana empire. In addition there had been waves of peaceful Manding settlers to this area, and the new conquest merely reinforced Manding influence and resulted in the foundation of a number of satellite kingdoms along the Gambia and in the interior of what is now Guinea Bissau. The latter provided a link with the coastal populations south of the Gambia who contributed kolanuts and other forest products to the markets of the Mali empire. This particular province, called Gabu or Cabo, gained importance as of the middle of the 15th century when the Portuguese started to establish trading stations along the Guinea Coast and its rivers. Early Portuguese sources confirm that these western provinces were ruled by a Manding vice-roy (*farin* in Manding) who was the representative of the 'king of kings' of Mali.[11]

The importance of the western provinces to the Mali empire has to be seen in the context of the threat of economic strangulation posed by Mali's diminishing control over trans-Saharan trade through the loss of the northern provinces. Since the contact with the Portuguese at various points along the Guinea Coast coincided with the weakening of central power, Gabo became virtually independent. By 1578 all Manding kingdoms of the Gambia, Casamance and the Guinean hinterland were vassals of the 'Farin Cabo', but the connection between this ruler and the king of Mali had apparently been severed. While Gabo was Manding dominated and had a substantial Manding population, it was essentially heterogeneous. Even as late as the 18th century more than 50% of the population of the Gambia were slaves of non-Manding origin (Quinn, 1972).

Yet despite the eventual isolation of this kingdom from its Manding source, the strong sense of Manding identity and the Manding system of centralised power seems to have favoured gradual language shift among the West Atlantic populations. That this process continued throughout the 19th century has been witnessed by many French and British travellers, who comment on the geographical spread of Manding and the ethnic groups most affected by language shift.[12]

The expansion of the Manding language in a southward direction also took place after the collapse of central power and was the result of gradual, more or less peaceful migrations, which occurred in response to the invasion of the north-eastern provinces. During the 15th, 16th and 17th centuries Manding traders and entire clans in search of cultivable land migrated south into what is now Burkina Faso, northern Ivory Coast and the interior of Guinea. This migration proceeded in stages, as a study of toponyms and clan names revealed, and it also involved assimilated Soninka clans (cf. Niane, 1975; and Person, 1964). Particularly the settlers who followed the Jula trade route from Jenne to Begho had a lasting influence on Manding language spread.

At each stage the same development can be observed: initially, Manding immigrants recognised the local power structure and entered into economic relations with the local population. Because of their extensive trade links the Jula merchants became popular negotiators between hostile ethnic groups and, through spreading Islam, they became the local authorities' councillors in juridical and religious matters. By the beginning of the 19th century, the Jula were in a position to seize political power as well, founding a number of kingdoms in this area and attracting great numbers of the local population who became assimilated.

Despite the disruptive events of the colonial period Jula has remained a stable, uniform dialect and has become the major lingua franca of this area. The still on-going process of language shift has been observed by sociolinguistic and other studies.[13]

Lastly, the military conquests of the Mali empire and the subsequent peaceful migrations of Manding people had another sociolinguistic consequence: that of the dislocation and dispersion of those neighbouring and related ethnolinguistic groups which resisted integration into the empire. Their fate is interesting in so far as it clearly demonstrates that isolation and separate social development are clearly linked to linguistic diversification and fragmentation, a subject we will turn to in Chapter 3.

During the three centuries of its existence the Mali empire had developed a system of centralised administration which survived, though on a smaller scale, in the various Manding states after the collapse of the empire. Why did this political fragmentation not result in greater linguistic fragmentation? The answer to this question leads us into an investigation of the social and cultural forces operating within Manding society.

Socio-cultural Identity and Language

African societies may be grouped into two broad categories: societies which are stratified and have a social organisation which transcends the village community, and societies which are egalitarian and organise their social life only within the village community, not recognising any authority beyond it. In stratified societies the social rank of the individual is fixed by birth through his membership of a specific clan or lineage. Such societies have a centre of power—a tribal chief—and a more or less complex hierarchical structure, and they may incorporate other tribal units through conquest and alliances and develop some of the characteristics of a feudal society.

This basic distinction according to social organisation is important for sociolinguistics because it affects not only language development and language use, but also the symbolic function of language. As we shall see in Chapter 3, in autonomous village societies (also called 'stateless') the symbolic function of language is to serve as a means of primary identification: specific linguistic features mark an individual as a member of a particular community which is also defined by the territory it occupies. The primary identity function of language retains its importance in larger stratified societies but, in addition, there is a secondary symbolic function: language becomes a deliberate tool in the struggle to maintain social cohesion and preserve the power structure. This aspect was particularly well developed in Manding society and preserved its language from the common fate of fragmentation.

Manding sociocultural identity was built on two pillars: one was language, the other was membership of a clan. It seems that Manding people have been language conscious since the early days of the Mali empire, since the Sunjata Epic gives a linguistic definition of who belonged to the Manding alliance.[14] Clan membership was recognisable by a common name and totem and, originally, clans were linked to a specific territory (province) with its chief bearing the title 'mansa'. In old Manding this chief ruled in conjunction with his council of elders and access to leadership depended on the degree of kinship with the ancestral founder of the clan. In the context of the Mali empire, however, clan membership also began to indicate social status: freemen were subdivided into occupational castes, such as cultivators, traders, metal workers, etc. and slaves were likewise subdivided, but belonged to the clan of their owners.

In its main features Manding social organisation is identical to that found in other major ethnic groups of the region, in particular the Soninka, Fulbe, Wolof and Songhai societies. The latter three came onto the historical stage later than the Manding and, having come into contact with them, may have taken over their hierarchical system. However, what is important here is not where this system originated, but that it was common to these five ethnic groups, speaking languages belonging to three different language families. It suggests that there was *far greater sociocultural unity than could be deduced from the linguistic situation*, and it is likely that this contributed more to inter-ethnic mobility, assimilation and language shift than any other factor. This is also suggested by the existence of a system of correspondence of clan names between these ethnic groups which is identifiable by a shared totem, and which implies that a member of a certain Wolof or Fulbe clan may adopt the Manding clan name while living in Manding territory, and vice versa. (15) While this custom may be no more than an expression of reciprocal hospitality, it could also serve as a means of assimilation and language shift. Indeed, Griffeth (1971) found that in the area of western Burkina Faso there was a marked preference for Manding names among ethnic minorities who had recently been converted to Islam and spoke Manding (Jula) as second language. Thereby they seemed to signal their intention to become assimilated.

The reasons why, in practice, language shift and assimilation has generally been a one-way process in favour of Manding has to be sought in the historical power relations created by the Mali empire, which are still capable of lending social and linguistic prestige to Manding.

The secondary symbolic function of language: that of being a tool in the struggle for cohesion, had its origins in the new social organisation of the Mali empire. The ascendance of one mansa over his peers was precipitated by a military crisis: the neighbouring Manding mansas accepted Sunjata's leadership in what is described as a war of liberation against a commonly perceived oppressor. His victory must have been so overwhelming that the lesser clan chiefs relinquished the royal title to Sunjata who then proceeded to a redistribution of territory and a redefinition of the rights and obligations of the principal Manding clans. This step represented a greater centralisation of power in the original Manding territories and an extension of Manding rule over non-Manding provinces. The latter were placed in an inferior social position, but likewise integrated into Manding society.

The key to the cohesive force of language, and hence to the extraordinary sense of cultural identity of the Manding people, their pride in their language and their history, is the royal bard—'jeli' in Manding. Actually, every clan had its jeli (also called griot or praise singer) whose main function it was to recite poems and songs celebrating the glorious deeds of the clan's ancestor and other famous members. However, this was not done in order to entertain: it was to remind particularly the young members of the clan of their social status, their rights and obligations, and thus was an important tool to reinforce the social order.

The royal jeli was recognised by Arab travellers as having an important function at the court. They referred to him alternately as 'interpreter', 'poet' or 'ambassador', though in fact he was a lot more than that. Above all the jeli was the king's chief counsellor and master of ceremonies; he was also court historian, retainer of tradition, interpreter of traditional law and principles of government and, last but not least, the educator of future kings.

The jeli's epics of the past glories of the Manding people are a fusion of literature, legend, moral teaching and historical fact, but above all *they are the most important tool of socialisation, formation of cultural identity and cohesion.* The jeli's greatest pride is his memory and the purity of his language—pure both in the sense of linguistic purity and truthfulness. His profession is passed on from father to son and his training, even today, involves long years of apprenticeship, travel and study in the various cultural centres of Manding, where his teachers watch over the accuracy of accent, intonation and the precise rendering of archaic rhetorical phrases. On becoming 'belen tigi' (master of the word) the jeli swears an oath that he will 'teach what there is to teach and keep silent what there is to be kept silent'.

What Ibn Battuta witnessed and related in his description of court audiences was the jeli relaying the king's words so that the latter would be spared the indignity of having to shout. Even when there is no need to shout, repetition of the same phrase by a mediator emphasises authority and underlines the public nature of a communication, in contrast to direct, private communication. Especially by couching the communication into an *appropriate* formalised speech style, the jeli reactivates the social hierarchy between speaker and listener and reaffirms law and order. Hence the institution of the jeli emphasises the secondary symbolic function of language by maintaining control over linguistic variation. His influence on language stability and the cultivation of a widely accepted standard cannot be underestimated, particularly in the context of expansion and contact with other languages.

To sum up: the development of Manding from a tribal language to one of West Africa's major lingua francas demonstrates the importance of non-linguistic factors for language spread. In this case the environmental conditions favoured communication and the development of trade. These in turn contributed to the establishment of a stable state formation, the conquest of new territories inhabited by other ethnolinguistic groups and the creation of a multi-ethnic and multilingual empire. Manding spread to the new dominions primarily as a lingua franca and, to the extent that political and economic integration was reinforced by Manding colonisation and the establishment of trading centres, the speakers of neighbouring languages were assimilated and adopted Manding as their first language.

Furthermore, the degree of linguistic stability and uniformity of the Manding language were also influenced by those factors, but here social organisation, cohesion and a very developed sense of socio-cultural and linguistic identity played the most important role. This combination of factors placed Manding in a unique position in that part of West Africa, though later events, such as the turbulent centuries of slave trade and the colonial conquest created obstacles and effectively halted further development and expansion until recently.

During my research on Manding language spread I was repeatedly struck by the coincidence that the forest fringe and the swampy coastal belt of the two Guineas and Sierra Leone marked the limit of Manding influence, though there is evidence of trade contacts. Some related ethnolinguistic groups, originally neighbours, seem to have rejected integration into the Mali empire and were repeatedly dislocated by its expansion. Their present linguistic distance is due to lack of contact with Manding and the influence of other languages with which they came into contact, as well as isolation from one another. They now inhabit the area which Dalby (1978) refers to as the 'linguistic fragmentation belt', along with many other ethnolinguistic groups which are small and highly fragmented. If the link between environment, social and linguistic development is to be established as a valid theory it should apply equally well to conditions which are, in every sense, the opposite to those described in this chapter.

Notes to Chapter 2

1. The following is the list of Mande languages as published by Dalby (1978). In his notation the two digits followed by a capital letter indicate a dialect cluster, a colon means 'the same as', a dash indicates inter-intelligibility and a comma a break in the dialect continuum: 31A Soso — Yalonka — Jalonka, Manding: Kagoro — Bamana — Khasonka — Mandinka — Maninka — Jakhanka — Wasulunka — Kuranko — Lele — Konyaka — Mauka — Jula, Kono — Vai, Ligbi. 31B Soninka — Marka — Azayr — Bozo. 31C Loko — Mende — Bandi, Loma, Kpelle, 31D Man, Dan, Tura, Mwa — Nwa — Gan — Kweni — Gban, 31E San, Bisa, Busa — Shanga, 31F Sya.

   All Manding scholars agree on the importance of the four central Manding dialects: *Maninka*, spoken in and around the Manding heartland on the Upper Niger, *Mandinka*, spoken in the Gambia, Guinea Bissau and southern Senegal, *Bamana* (or *Bambara*) spoken in Mali, and *Jula* (also spelled Dyula or Dioula), spoken in Burkina Faso and Ivory Coast.

2. cf. Levtzion & Hopkins (1981), which contains all of the Arab sources cited. Al-Bakri relates that the conversion of the king of Malel was brought about through a severe drought—possibly the same which is referred to in a Soninka legend which led to the collapse of the empire of Ghana and the dispersion of its people (Delafosse, 1913).

3. cf. Niane (1960) '[the Soninka] are great merchants, their heavily laden donkey caravans came in every dry season up to Niani; they established themselves behind the city and the inhabitants came out to barter with them'. (p.64, author's translation)

4. cf. Person (1971), also Goody (1964) and Wilks (1962).

5. Levtzion & Hopkins (1981) Note that Ibn Khaldoun mentions Sunjata under the name 'Mari-Jata', the lion prince, which is one of his titles used in oral tradition. He also comments on the Manding system of succession, which was matrilinear despite conversion to Islam.

6. Levtzion & Hopkins, 1981: 273. 'Sudan' literally means 'the black people' and was also used to refer to the entire sub-Saharan region of Africa.

7. This observation by the French traveller Mouette (1683) is quoted by Sundstrom (1974: 24).

8. Later sources give information on markets further south as far as the Sierra Leone hinterland, but the only indication of their connection with the Manding network is the title 'farim' given to their rulers. cf. Brooks (1980).

9. According to Wright (1977) the Jakhanka of the Gambia were originally Soninka, but adopted Manding once the Gambia was dominated by the Mali empire. cf. also Person (1971) on the Turé and Cissé clans in the area of Kankan in Guinea.

10. Levtzion & Hopkins (1981: 335). cf. also comments concerning Manding language use and language shift to Manding, particularly among people speaking related Mande languages (McCall, 1971; Calvet, 1982).

11. Teixeira da Mota (1978) cites a reference by the 16th century merchant Almada to the king of the Casamance, 'a vassal of the Farim Cabo, who in his turn owes allegiance to the Mandimansa, the emperor of the blacks'.

12. cf. Park (1799), Mollien (1820) and Bocandé (1849). Mollien reported that Gabu (i.e. the country between the Gambia and the Rio Geba) was inhabited by a mixed population, but that the Manding were in the majority and their language was the only one used. Similarly, Bocandé comments that 'the Balanta who are the closest to the Manding, have changed their language and customs: they no longer want to be considered Balanta and call themselves Manding'.

13. Griffeth (1971) describes the present social and cultural prestige of the Jula in Burkina Faso, where conversion to Islam is usually accompanied by the adoption of a Manding name and eventual language shift. He also quotes L.G. Binger (1892: 394) 'when one knows how to speak Mande it is very rare not to find persons who can serve you as interpreters—regardless where one travels in this vast region'.

14. cf. Niane (1960: 160): 'All the sons of Manding were there, all those who say n'ko, all those who speak the clear Manding language'. To this he adds: 'n'ko means I say in Manding. Manding people like to differentiate themselves from other people by their language; for them Manding is the *clear language* (Kangbe) par excellence. All those who say n'ko are, in principle, Manding'.

15. cf. Niane (1984a) on clan correspondences: Manding clan Condé = Wolof clan Ndiaye; Manding clan Traoré = Wolof clan Diop; Manding clan Keita = Fulbe clan Ba = Soninka clan Cissé; cf. also Ly-Tall (1984) on the same phenomenon concerning Songhai clans.

3 Linguistic Fragmentation in the West African Coastal Belt

The contrast between the environment of the Sahel and savanna zones and that of the Upper Guinea Coast could not be greater. Instead of the wide open plains of the interior where human settlements are only separated by distance we have low lying marshes and mangrove swamps, broken up by meandering rivers and large estuaries which dissect the coast line into quasi-islands and actual off-shore islands. Geographers refer to this phenomenon as the *drowned coast*. The population inhabiting this semi-amphibious zone is often living in extreme isolation, and the frequently insanitary conditions impose serious limitations to population growth. In many places the coastal swamps merge into dense forests which, while they might occasionally support a higher population density, still impose barriers to communication and thus favour the social pattern of small autonomous village societies.

Although there is a certain amount of linguistic continuity, in the sense that languages belong either to the West Atlantic or Mande language families, physical isolation and socio-historical conditions have contributed to considerable linguistic fragmentation. Many languages are spoken by a very small number of speakers, restricted to one or a few villages, and slightly more substantial ethnolinguistic groups are broken up into small communities speaking different dialects.

As outlined in Chapter 2, the Manding trade network created a continuous chain of statelets on both sides of the Gambia, joining these to the Gabu states in the south. However, Manding rule south of the Gambia did not extend to the Atlantic coast but stopped about 50–150 kilometres inland. The mangrove swamps, marshlands and inter-connecting tidal channels to the west with their malaria bearing mosquitos and tsetse flies effectively halted the westward advance of the Manding conquerors and their cavalry. In Guinea Bissau three great river systems have created deep fjords, swamps and flood zones in the coastal belt. In addition there is the

Bissagos Island Archipelago with numerous large and small islands scattered along the coast. Here too Manding expansion extended only over the savanna interior: the western-most trading posts of the Gabu network, where trade with the Portuguese caravels took place, were situated at the head of navigation on each of the three rivers—the Cacheu, the Geba and the Corubal.

The four West African countries south of the Gambia: Senegal (Casamance), Guinea Bissau, Guinea and Sierra Leone have part of their territory in this coastal zone and hence share this sociolinguistic peculiarity of fragmentation or *horizontal multilingualism*. While the interior formed part of the Manding complex, the coastal areas have served as a refuge for diverse splinter groups which, thanks to their isolation, were able to resist integration.

Environmental Impact on Social and Linguistic Development

However linguists may define the distinction between language and dialect there can be no doubt as to the correlates of linguistic variation: the more isolated a community lives from its neighbours, the more its language is likely to develop along different lines, even if at the outset the neighbouring varieties shared the same linguistic features. Furthermore, fostering linguistic variation may be an expression of the community's politico-cultural purpose and its sense of identity.

The linguistic classification which best expresses the sociolinguistic characteristics of the West African coastal belt is the set system developed by Dalby (1978), as it represents in digits the degree of relationship between them. The following is a list of ten locations on the Guinea Coast (from north to south) and the languages spoken in that area, with their set identification according to Dalby.[1]

(1) Gambia river to Guinea Bissau border: Joola 22A, Manjaku 22B, Banun 23C.
(2) Guinea Bissau border to Cacheu river: Joola 22A, Manjaku 22B, Papel 22B, Banun 23C.
(3) Cacheu river to Bissau and off-shore islands: Manjaku 22B, Papel 22B.
(4) Bissau to Guinea border: Balanta 22C, Biafada 23B, Mankanya 22B, Biafada 23B, Balanta 22C, Nalu 24.
(5) Bissagos Archipelago and other off-shore islands: Bijogo 205, Biafada 23B.
(6) Guinea border to north of Konakry: Nalu 24, Landuma 25A, Baga 25A.
(7) Central coast and Konakry: Susu 31A.
(8) Border area Guinea/Sierra Leone: Mmani 25B, Susu 31A.

(9) Northern Sierra Leone to Freetown: Limba 206, Temne 25A, Bullom 25B, Kru 26, Krio (Portuguese Creole).

(10) South of Freetown: Mende 31C, Krim 25B, Vai 31A.

The repetition in this list is due to the phenomenon of linguistic islands, generally corresponding to geographical features, namely a territory bordered by rivers, swamps, etc. or the fact that past migratory movements of a different ethnolinguistic group drove a wedge between the previously contiguous territories of the original population.

Dalby's system of sets is purely synchronic, thus side-stepping the issue of historical development and the fragmentation process (which language split up into which dialects or languages). However, as in most cases we now have information about the percentage of common vocabulary which is shared by related languages, this can be analysed scientifically and related to the degree of isolation. There is also the quantitative aspect: small splinter groups (such as the Banun 23C) having lived in isolation for a long time, tend to opt for language shift when in contact with a larger ethnolinguistic group. In other words, there seems to be a point at which language divergence and fragmentation will ultimately lead to the extinction of such languages.

One of the best researched languages of the above listed West Atlantic languages is Joola, spoken in the Casamance district of Senegal and in Guinea Bissau. The Senegalese Joola inhabit an area which stretches from the Atlantic coast to the district capital Ziguinchor on both sides of the Casamance river. During the last part of its course this river has a wide and deep bed, winding its way through marshy country. Sea water rises up to 150 kilometres inland and the pressure of the tides has created a multitude of large and small waterways bordered by mangrove swamps, in the midst of which there are fertile islands and semi-islands. Some of the villages are accessible only by canoe, others by dirt tracks (negotiable only during the dry season), and larger channels have to be crossed by canoe or ferry. Until recently, these small agricultural communities had a subsistence economy and only marginal trade contacts.

The language map of this area (Atlas du Sénégal, 1977) registers twelve small linguistic communities, usually grouped under the ethnic label *Joola*, as well as a number of scattered Banun and Manjak communities. Eight of these Joola dialects are inter-intelligible, but four others have acquired very different linguistic features and are now considered to be separate languages.[2] These appear to be a particularly clear example for the role of the environment in linguistic fragmentation.

The first of these Joola splinter languages—*Bayot*—has a number of very distinct phonological and morphological features which separate it from

Joola. The people speaking this language live in the dense forest completely surrounded by tidal channels. This was once impenetrable virgin forest which afforded unique protection in times of insecurity—in particular during the slave raids and tribal warfare of the last centuries. In response to this environment the Bayot adapted their habitat and their agricultural techniques. In contrast to the often substantial villages elsewhere in this part of Casamance, the Bayot village consists of tiny scattered hamlets, hidden in the forest and linked only by narrow paths. Theirs is an extreme degree of social fragmentation with only a minimum of interaction within a very small radius, and no visible form of social discipline. Each one-family-hamlet is essentially autonomous, cultivating a small garden and a few nearby clearings in the forest, and supplementing their own products with forest crops such as palm oil and fruit. Population density is relatively low (18 inhabitants per square kilometre) but stable, and the 1960 census registered 5600 Bayot inhabitants.[3]

Kwatay is the language spoken in the village Diembering and three other villages situated on a narrow strip of coastal dunes south of the Casamance estuary. These dunes are separated from the mainland by a large channel and an intricate network of large and small creeks. The language maps of Sapir (1965) and Doneux (1977) identify the southern tip of this sand bar with the large village Kabrousse as the territory of yet another variety called *Her*. Until recently there was no road link and the physical barriers mentioned above effectively isolated these villages. Linguists estimate that Kwatay is spoken by about 4000 people and Her by 2000–3000.

The last of these splinter languages—*Karon*—seems to be an off- shoot of Kwatay and is mainly spoken in the village Kafountine and on two estuary islands. This is the most fragmented and most inaccessible part of the Casamance estuary, with islands consisting of narrow sand bars, surrounded entirely by a labyrinth of mangrove swamps and tidal chan-nels. There are only a few scattered villages and population density is only about 8 inhabitants per square kilometre. In the largest of the villages where Karon is spoken (Kafountine, north of the Casamance river) there is a marked influence of Manding language spread from Gambia, and grad-ual language shift from Karon to Manding has been observed since the fifties and sixties. In fact, the phenomenon of language shift has been increasing among all the speakers of these Joola splinter languages over the last 30 years, since their isolation has been diminishing.

Environmental conditions alone obviously do not suffice to produce linguistic fragmentation, since the impact of the environment does not act directly upon language use, but indirectly through its impact on society. There are many examples of societies where internal social organisation and historical events have succeeded in counteracting the impact of the environment. In the case of the Joola, however, history and social organisation have tended to reinforce the isolating impact of the environment.

Social Organisation and Language Use in Autonomous Village Societies

As mentioned in Chapter 2 the social organisation of Manding society with its strict social hierarchy created a situation in which language is part of a sophisticated set of social rules which act in unison to maintain social and linguistic cohesion. Autonomous village societies are organised communally and, even when neighbouring villages belong to the same ethnolinguistic group, they recognise no authority beyond the village chief. The traditional Joola communities—those who speak inter-intelligible dialects and those referred to as *splinter groups*—are a typical example for this kind of social organisation.

As elsewhere, kinship is the basic unit of organisation, but here there was, and partly still is, complete equality: there were neither slaves, nor artisan castes nor ruling families. Some villages had chiefs whose function was, however, primarily ritual and whose authority was based neither on the rank of the person nor on the institution as such, but on personality. The chief was merely the wisest or the most courageous, chosen from among the elders, and had to maintain his position against constant competition. Other villages were ruled by a council of elders on the basis of common consent, and in the final analysis it was always in this group that real authority was vested. The only type of social differentiation in these communities was related to age groups: with initiation into adulthood, and each promotion into a higher age group, the individuals of the group were given higher responsibilities in community life and hence gained in prestige. However, both the obligations and the privileges were shared by all members of the group. Property rights over cattle and the use of land were vested in the family and the head of each family used to make an annual distribution of land use among the male adults, to each according to his needs.

Relationship between villages, particularly if they belonged to different clans, were competitive and mostly hostile in the past. Only between old villages and their daughter settlements was there a recognised bond, but as these were often at great distances from one another, it was more of a cultural bond and had no practical implications. In practice each village was responsible for its own survival and defense. This isolation both reflects the situation as imposed by the environment and reinforces the effects of isolation.

Linguistic fragmentation can only be enhanced in a situation where physical contact is both difficult and discouraged by the social order. Minor dialect differences become crucial when they are linked to the distinction between friend and foe. Even today, the problem of inter-intelligibility between the dialects and languages of this group should be approached with caution. There is a very common social rule of language behaviour which transforms the individual's psycho-social reaction to an outsider into a linguistic reaction ('I don't understand his speech'), thereby avoiding the responsibility for a communicative act which may be interpreted as a transgression. This is particularly the case in a social setting where, traditionally, social initiative belongs to the group and its representative rather than to the individual. There are examples in sociolinguistic literature of neighbouring village societies communicating through an interpreter, despite the fact that to the outsider their forms of speech are virtually identical.[4]

In this context it is useful to return to the subject of silent trade. The small agricultural communities of the Guinea coast and forest regions had essentially a subsistence economy and only some of these produced a tradable commodity, namely the cola nut. As with the gold trade, it always was the aim of the socially stratified trading societies to exclude the producers from direct trade contacts through the system of silent barter. From the point of view of the producers' societies the social rule against linguistic contact likewise served to protect their interests, preserved their secrets and kept intact their sociolinguistic identity.

Another aspect which distinguishes the communally organised, stateless societies from stratified societies like the Manding is their absence of a sense of history; or rather the phenomenon that traditions preserved orally are limited to each village, concern exclusively the village founder and are to be understood more in a mythical-cultic sense. Ancestor worship forms part of the animist cult of these societies and in this context one can observe, among Joola societies for instance, that special relationships between two or three villages exist which are traceable to the establishment of new villages. And yet, despite this particularism, Joola societies appear to have an awareness that they belong to the same cultural unit.

What this awareness is based on is difficult to assess as historical references on this subject are scarce. On the basis of a 15th century Portuguese source mentioning the Joola as inhabitants of the Gambia estuary and the Atlantic coast to the south of it, Quinn (1972) suggests that the Joola were the original population of the Gambia valley and had, at some stage, a greater political organisation . The influx of Manding migration into the Gambia in the 14th and 15th century is thought to have destroyed this and forced the Joola further south into the swamps and forests of the Casamance estuary up to the Cacheu River. In the 16th century one of their sub-units, the *Falup*, inhabiting then the southern shore of the Casamance is mentioned by Fernandes.

According to this evidence their social and linguistic fragmentation appears to be the result of the combined influence of defeat at the hands of the Manding, persecution during the slave raids and the environment. Indeed, both the choice of the environment and fragmentation may be interpreted as a more or less conscious protective measure.

One thing does seem certain: ever since the arrival of the Portuguese traders on the Atlantic coast, the Joola communities inhabiting this zone have been in constant conflict, particularly with Manding communities who, as intermediaries for the Portuguese, traded in the products of the hinterland and conducted slave raids. While the Joola were not averse to trading as such, they were hostile to the Manding approach which sought to exert direct influence and eventually integrate the less organised societies with which they came into contact.

There can be no doubt that in these adverse conditions the Joola communities were greatly protected by the impenetrable nature of their environment and, paradoxically, by the absence of any political organisation beyond the village level. This is can also be demonstrated by the late and extremely difficult establishment of colonial rule in this area—according to Roche (1976) it took the French 75 years to subdue the people of the Casamance. In other words, in conjunction with the environment, the social organisation of autonomous village communities was of great survival value under the conditions prevailing in the past four centuries.

Fragmentation and Language Shift Among Small Stratified Societies

The various social forces which contributed to the spread of the Manding language and its resistance to fragmentation may be taken as a yardstick by which to measure processes leading to the opposite result. One of these cohesive forces was the Manding system of social organisation which clearly defined the social hierarchy of its members and the authority of the tribal chief. Yet there were limits to this cohesive sociolinguistic force which, in fact, coincided with the limits of Manding central power. Populations which did not recognise the authority of the king of Mali, no matter how closely related their languages may originally have been to Manding, engaged on a road to separate development. A combination of deliberate isolation, contact with other languages plus the element of time produced diversification and fragmentation of the southern Mande languages and a

few distant Manding dialects. Their communities were the original inhabitants of the forest zones of Guinea and Ivory Coast, neighbours of the Mali
empire, who provided the Manding trade network with cola nuts and other
forest products. They are likely to be identical with those forest 'barbarians'
described in the Arab sources[5] who rejected both Manding rule and Islam,
but had a similar social structure. Their separateness became enhanced
when the Mali empire slowly extended its influence further south and
entire Manding clans migrated in search of cultivable land. As a result
these distant cousins had to choose between integration and migration;
some of them ended up in the dense forests of Ivory Coast, and others near
the border between Guinea, Sierra Leone and Liberia.

A parallel development, though less extreme, accounts for a number of
distant dialects of Manding. While collecting data on the migration of
Manding clans, Person (1964 and 1984) came across historical and linguistic
evidence that parts of northern Ivory Coast and the immediately adjacent
region of Guinea were originally inhabited by people speaking a different
dialect. These he identified as the *Ligbi*—a small remnant group inhabiting
the western Volta region of Ghana—and the *Vai* and *Kono* of Sierra Leone.
According to Dalby (1978) these speak remote dialects of Manding. Manding scholars link the Ligbi migration to the Jula trade route from Jenne to
the Gold Coast, where they maintained contact with central Manding for
some time. The Vai and Kono are thought to have been connected with the
trade route from the Upper Niger to the Atlantic coast. The presence of the
Vai (though under a different name) is mentioned in early Portuguese
sources, hence they must have been settled in their present location (the
border region between Sierra Leone and Liberia) by the middle of the 15th
century.

What makes these three ethnolinguistic groups interesting is that their
participation in the two mentioned trade networks preserved them from a
greater degree of diversification. In fact, Portuguese sources comment on
the similarity of the Vai language and social structure with that of the
Manding of the Gambia. They also refer to other Manding-related groups,
invading Liberia and Sierra Leone during the 15th and 16th century, which
resulted partly in a social transformation of some West Atlantic societies
but, perhaps more importantly, their intrusion created linguistic enclaves
and separated a number of West Atlantic groups from their previous
neighbours, thereby speeding up linguistic fragmentation.

Another cause for linguistic fragmentation and language shift among
small stratified societies can be demonstrated particularly well in connection with three ethnolinguistic groups inhabiting the coastal belt of Guinea
Bissau: the *Balanta*, the *Biafada* and the *Banun*. These speakers of West

Atlantic languages were mentioned by Portuguese traders and later French travellers[6] as communities of considerable size and economic importance, yet, contrary to expectation, their development has been a negative one. One of these languages has virtually disappeared and the others are spoken only in scattered communities and the number of their speakers is shrinking.

The Balanta appear to have been connected with the Manding state of Gabu since its foundation—they made up the majority of the original population, conquered by a group of Manding warriors. The latter, according to oral tradition, brought with them a Manding princess who married the Balanta king. What is certain is that the names of the two royal lineages are not Manding and that, unlike in later Manding society, kingship in Gabu was determined by matrilinear descent. However, in this apparent arrangement of power sharing the Balanta language and identity was the loser. Large sections of the population became fully assimilated into Manding society and abandoned the language of their ancestors. This process of language shift continued throughout the centuries[7] and the remaining Balanta speakers appear to be those whose ancestors refused integration.

A similar fate befell the Biafada who, in the 16th century, occupied one third of the territory of present Guinea Bissau. They figure largely in the accounts of Almada[8] who described the socio-economic situation of the Upper Guinea coast in the 1570s. Almada lists a number of Biafada kingdoms, some having a mixed Biafada and Manding population, but all subject to the 'farim Cabo', the Manding vice-roy. Their main economic role was to transport cola from the Nunez river in their large dug-out canoes to the major Manding cola market on the Upper Geba, a network which is likely to have existed in pre-Manding times. Because of their knowledge of the water ways and boat building experience, the Biafada were later on employed as navigators and intermediaries for the Luso-African traders, the descendants of Portuguese mariners and Africans from the Cape Verde Islands. The decline of this apparently substantial and commercially active ethnic group began in the 17th century with the establishment of Luso-African communities in Bissau and Cacheu, which attracted trade away from them, and with their acceptance of playing a subservient role. Being placed between two economically powerful groups—the Manding and the Luso-Africans—most of the Biafada were assimilated into one or the other of these groups and only a remnant of about 12,000 people are estimated as using this language.

The historical development of the Banun (also called *Bainuk*) followed a similar pattern. These seem to have established a trade network linking the estuaries of the rivers Cacheu, Casamance and Gambia via connecting tidal channels and tributaries. Portuguese sources (Almada and Donelha) mention five Banun kingdoms and describe a fierce conflict lasting 35 years (1545–1580) between the northern Banun and Joola on the one hand and the 'Cassamansa', a Manding ruler, on the other. This has been interpreted as a kind of battle of independence against Manding overlordship or an economic war with each party attempting to establish a trading monopoly with the Luso-Africans (Brooks, 1980). It was won by the Banun and Joola and, as of 1590 the former gave Luso-African traders permission to settle in their territory (Ziguinchor on the Casamance river). While this special relationship with the Luso-Africans appears to have strengthened the Banun position throughout the 17th century, it was followed by rapid decline. The Luso-Africans settled in African coastal communities between Sierra Leone and Gambia and served as middlemen in Euro-African trading relations[9].

The tide began to turn in the 17th century with more Portuguese arriving, establishing fortified trading stations at Cacheu, Ziguinchor and Bissau, and missionary activities undermining Guinean societies from within. (It is noteworthy that Manding rulers did not permit Portuguese settlements in their realms and that Manding trade continued to flourish until the colonial conquest at the very end of the 19th century.) A great proportion of the Banun population were absorbed into the Creole population and speak the language which developed as a result of Afro-Portuguese contact and inter-marriage: *Crioulo*. From the mid-19th century there are French records mentioning still substantial Banun communities between the Gambia and Casamance rivers, but one hundred years later they had shrunk to about 12,000 in both colonies. In Senegal the 1976 census no longer lists the Banun as a distinct ethnic group, although linguists estimate that about 2000 people scattered among the Joola population still speak this language.

In this particular case the process of language shift is almost complete: poverty forces most of the sons and daughters of those few Banun speaking families to leave their villages to seek work in town where inter-ethnic marriage is unavoidable. Thus even the last social function—that of being the intimate language of the home—disappears, and without a social function no language can remain alive.

In some of the cases discussed in this chapter it seems clear that language expansion and its opposite—the slow process of extinction— may be simply two sides of the same coin. The gain of one language is the loss of another. The main factors behind such changes are usually primarily socio-economic, but it seems equally clear that the survival of small fragmented language communities is linked to environmental conditions.

Without an isolating type of environment the weaker societies would have succumbed to the stronger much sooner. As it is the aim of all social organisation to serve the survival of the group, no matter what size, the patterns of language use reflect a conservative tendency until such time as a given social unit loses its cohesive force and the individual's concern for survival is no longer identical with that of the group.

However, it seems that the persistence of linguistic fragmentation in this part of West Africa is due to other factors which, so far, have only been touched upon briefly: the effects of the contact of African societies with the economically and militarily more powerful European trading partners which eventually resulted in subjugation and colonisation. These events may not appear to have a direct relationship with language but, as I hope to demonstrate in the following chapter, the events which perturbed and, in some cases, destroyed or profoundly changed African societies deprived African languages of the social conditions necessary for their full development. They also introduced new factors which added to the degree of linguistic diversity in African countries.

Notes to Chapter 3

1. In this system two digits indicate a complex set—a language group with a close overall relationship—and the letter placed after the digits indicates a subset. Three digits signify that a language so labelled does not fit into any of the other sets. The initial digit (2) refers to West Atlantic languages while (3) refers to Mande languages.
2. cf. Doneux (1978) and personal communication.
3. The 1976 census of Senegal makes no mention of these splinter groups and I have been informed that they were incorporated into the Joola group.
4. cf. among others, the research done on mutual intelligibility and attitudes in Zambia and Uganda (Chapter 2, Note 3) which revealed that statements concerning intelligibility frequently contradicted objective linguistic evidence.
5. There are several references to the *Zanj*, eaters of human flesh, but a more significant anecdote concerning the forest neighbours of the Manding is told by Al-Umari: when Mansa Musa was asked during his visit to Cairo, why he had not converted the heathens of his gold producing provinces and made them direct subjects of his empire, he replied that an attempt to convert them had proved to have such negative results (a drastic decline in the yield of gold) that it had to be abandoned.
6. Brooks (1980) cites the French traveller La Courbe, who followed the Banun network from the Gambia to the Cacheu river in 1686.
7. cf. the comment by Bocande (1849) quoted in Note 12 to Chapter 2.
8. The accounts of Almada and other Portuguese merchants and travellers concerning the people of the Guinea coast are frequently cited by Teixeira da Mota (1978) and Brooks (1980).
9. cf. Brooks (1980) on the role of the Luso-Africans (lancados).

4 Arrested Development and Regression

Historically speaking, this chapter begins where Chapter 2 ended, as it raises a number of questions concerning the sociolinguistic development in the geographical area of the Mali empire after its demise. Two events at the close of the 16th century provoked the collapse of this multi-ethnic empire in which the economic, social and cultural influence of the Manding had created a tendency towards assimilation and unification. Firstly, the Portuguese succeeded in diverting a great part of the gold trade between the Volta bend and Timbuktu towards Elmina (Gold Coast) where they established a trading fort. Secondly, the hostilities between the Songhai and Morocco in the north resulted in the destruction of Sijilmasa (the Saharan salt mines) as well as the trading centres Gao, Timbuktu and Jenne, which caused further rapid decline of trade along the western trans-Saharan route.

The combined effect of these two events gave the already weakened Mali empire a final blow and it broke down into several parts. A much reduced Manding kingdom remained on the Upper Niger under the rule of the old Manding dynasty. Other small Manding kingdoms became independent (in particular those on the Middle Niger—Segu and Kaarta) while the western provinces, reconstituted as the empire of Gabu, gained in economic importance because of its position on the Atlantic. The vassal kingdoms of non-Manding origin also became independent and new states were founded, all of them ethno-centric in their outlook and engaged in a constant struggle for supremacy. In other words, the homogenising influence of the Mali empire, with its use of a common lingua franca, was replaced by a tendency towards social fragmentation and increased linguistic heterogeneity.

The Sociolinguistic Consequences of the Slave Trade

This then was the internal situation at the time when European traders discovered the enormous profitability of the slave trade. While this is not the place for a discussion concerning the economic effects of the slave trade on African societies[1] there can be no doubt that it caused immeasurable social upheaval and had far reaching sociolinguistic consequences.

A society which sells its own labour force has no economic future and, in fact, African societies rarely sold their own slaves. Certain elements within some of these societies, however, were induced or forced by slave traders to raid neighbouring societies in order to obtain a renewable supply of that commodity which was increasingly in demand: the human person. The slave trade reached its peak in the 18th century, by which time not only the feudalistic states of the coast, but also those of the interior were almost exclusively engaged in conducting wars and slave raids to satisfy the growing demand for slaves in all Atlantic ports.

The major victims of the slave trade were the weaker societies, in particular the less organised, egalitarian village societies inhabiting the hinterland of the Atlantic coast.[2] Those who were not entirely wiped out continued a precarious existence in small groups in areas of refuge, such as the coastal marshes or other inaccessible places. The French traveller Mollien (1820) mentions 'remainders of great nations' living in the area around Bissau, having fled from the raiding parties of the Manding and the Fulbe during the previous centuries. He also comments on the area between the Futa Jallon and the Rio Grande, where he found the almost deserted, totally impoverished villages of the Tenda, who were the original inhabitants of most of the Gambia valley and the western slopes of the Futa Jallon. Only a few communities of this fragmented ethnic group survive today.[3] These few surviving villages of a formerly much more numerous group owe their existence to this mountain refuge, but it is predictable that they will not be able to preserve their identity for much longer, since their only hope for survival in the modern context lies in migration, assimilation and language shift.[4]

In addition to population decimation through export, the slaving activities of the 18th century led to internal deportations and migrations, resulting in the kind of ethno-linguistic confusion as described by Suret-Canale (1973:132):

> neighbouring villages belong to different ethnic groups—here the descendants of first occupants, there the conquerors and there refugees chased from their original habitat or captives deposited by the conquest.

Eye witnesses like Mungo Park and Mollien also mention a new phenomenon, that of slave villages, of which they saw many examples in the Manding and Fulbe states between the Gambia and the Niger, as well as in Futa Jallon. These were villages where the victims of raids were temporarily parked and where, until such time as a caravan would be organised leaving for the coast, or while waiting for the slavers' ships, the captives were employed as cultivators and artisans. When the slave trade eventually started to decline, such slave villages became the main centres of assimilation, where a mixed population adopted the language of their masters.[5] While in these cases language shift eventually created homogeneous communities, the survival of small splinter groups in the zones of refuge considerably added to the multilingual situation in those parts, as we have seen in Chapter 3.

The Establishment of Colonial Rule: Divide and Conquer

Efforts at penetration and military conquest by the colonial powers increased during the second half of the 19th century and provoked a wave of violent resistance. Among these were two last-minute attempts at rallying and uniting various related groups, one around a strong Manding ruler, and the other around a Tukulor ruler.[6] Both were attempting to break down the privileges of tribal aristocracies and to lay the foundations of centralised states. Both were doomed to failure because they occurred simultaneously with the advance of the better equipped colonial armies, but also because ethnic rivalries and class divisions had become aggravated under the pressure of the slave trade and the colonial conquest. While the new Manding-Jula empire undoubtedly brought about a revival of Manding socio-cultural identity and increased the trend towards linguistic homogenisation in northern Ivory Coast, the Tukulor empire was unable to rally ethnic support and did not create any greater linguistic cohesion between the various Fulbe territories. However, had these two attempts at state formation succeeded, it is likely that the areas indicated on Map 4 (page 69) would have become more integrated, both socially and linguistically. In this sense then we can describe the influence of the conquest as having arrested such a development, with all that this implies for language use and linguistic development.

However, there was more than arrested development; there was actual regression due to the dissolution of African state formations, the breakdown of the traditional social order and fragmentation of ethnolinguistic groups. One of the reasons was that military control over vast areas, achieved through the superiority of European arms, could only be maintained by the application of the principle *divide and conquer*, thus ensuring that the force of traditional ethnolinguistic loyalties or other cohesive forces were rendered inoperative. Colonial records frequently comment on the extent of tribal hostilities and internal rivalries in Africa, but while disguising the conquest as a *pacification* process, the new rulers were very skilful at exploiting these hostilities, at using Africans against Africans in order to conquer and then administer their colonies.[7] Greatly facilitating the installation of colonial rule, these methods generally resulted in the fragmentation of the larger political entities, and the destruction of the smaller ones.

This was particularly the case in the French territories, with their system of centralised and direct administration, while British attempts at indirect rule, notably in the Hausa/Fulani emirates of northern Nigeria, were comparatively less disruptive to the established social organisation and its pattern of language use. Furthermore, the vast and almost contiguous French territories were arbitrarily subdivided into at first five, then eight separately administered colonies. In each case the borders of these colonies (and it is difficult to believe that this was not a deliberate policy) *cut across ethnolinguistic entities while enclosing a number of traditionally hostile groups*. As a consequence each colony was composed of such a bewildering number of ethnic groups that, even if it had been their policy to encourage the use and development of local languages, this would have presented quite a problem. As it was, French policy led to the suppression and dialectalisation of the local languages and aimed at imposing French as the unique language of public communication.

The more or less forced population movements were another cause for fragmentation. While centuries of slave trade had provoked quite a number of migrations, creating greater linguistic heterogeneity in the less accessible parts of West Africa, the population movements resulting from the colonial conquest were unequalled in African history, both in extent and in intensity. Unlike the slave trade, they affected all parts of Africa and all types of societies.

In many parts of West Africa the advancing colonial armies left behind them burned villages, destroyed crops and populations decimated by wars and famine. Often the only solution for a leaderless, defeated population seemed to lie in escape to temporarily unaffected areas. Since these were often the same impenetrable forests, swamps and isolated mountain valleys which had previously served as refuge to populations escaping from the slave raiders, these migrations added to the linguistic diversity of such areas. They also triggered off waves of migration, such as the mass exodus of the Manding population loyal to Samori following the defeat of 1892, which followed the trail of his army across northern Ivory Coast into Burkina Faso and Ghana, in turn setting into motion the original inhabitants of those areas.

Other population movements were a form of protest against all kinds of repressive measures: forced labour, conscription into the colonial army and heavy taxation. Individual families of all ethnic groups fled from the

French territories into the as yet unconquered hinterland of Liberia and Sierra Leone. Others crossed the borders into British territories, particularly to evade tax and conscription and, in some cases, returned or moved on when they found that similar conditions prevailed there.

Although migrations were a frequent phenomenon in Africa, the sociolinguistic result of these population movements following the conquest were very different. Traditionally, migrations occurred within the framework of a social organisation, as entire tribes, clans or villages went in search of new land, resettled and, even if they were brought into contact with another ethnic group, were able to preserve their identity and maintain their languages. The protest migrations described above were far more chaotic and resulted in further social and linguistic fragmentation, leading to large scale language shift. Only in this case language shift was not necessarily in favour of one of the major lingua francas, but in favour of any language spoken in the marginalised zones which served as refuge.

A second form of migration continues until the present, which has temporarily created zones of very high linguistic diversity. These are the labour migrations which began in the 1920s from the poorer, undeveloped countries of the interior to the coastal zones where colonial investment was concentrated in plantations and urban development.

One of the more striking examples is the migration from Burkina Faso (formerly Upper Volta) to Ivory Coast and Ghana, distances of up to 2000 kilometers. It began as conscription of individual males from various ethnic groups in the 1920s, when Upper Volta was used as a labour pool. Between 1920 and 1970 the proportion of population density between the coast and the interior changed considerably. According to some sources[8] the foreign residents in some parts of Ivory Coast amount to 50%, whereas in Ghana the 1960 census listed over half a million foreign residents (from Upper Volta and Togo) working in the cocoa and coffee plantations of southern Ghana alone. These figures exclude the assimilated and naturalised citizens, and the total immigrant population since 1920 is estimated at 1.3 million in Ivory Coast and 2.3 million in Ghana. The colonial experiments with peanut cultivation in Gambia and Senegal, and rubber tapping in Guinea Bissau and Casamance (Senegal) had similar effects on the composition of the population, as in each case they introduced minority groups from other colonies, thereby increasing the number of languages spoken in these areas, and in many cases this was on a permanent basis.[9]

Labour migration in the colonial context had two motives: the main purpose was of course to move labour force to where it was needed, but since there seems to have been no shortage of labour in the south, the secondary motive was only thinly disguised. In fact, it served the deliberate policy of breaking up any remaining resistance of closely knit local communities by introducing aliens who would remain dependent on the colonial administration or European commercial companies. The most obvious sociolinguistic result of such a policy was increased linguistic diversity in the areas receiving immigrants on the one hand, and depletion of the zones from which labour was recruited on the other which, in some cases, left fragments of ethnic groups behind, whose languages joined the long list of languages which are no longer socially viable. It also increased the African labourers' reliance on the mediation of colonial officers and trading companies, and with it the need for some knowledge of French or English, or at any rate a pidginised version of these languages. It is therefore not surprising that southern Ivory Coast, being host to so many immigrants, was the only French colony in which a French pidgin evolved.

The Growth of Multilingual Urban Centres

Urbanisation is intimately related to the development of trade, and since West Africa has participated in long distance trade since the 8th century, urbanisation is not a new phenomenon, nor is the accompanying multilingual situation. However, the greatest urban centres of modern West Africa are not related to precolonial trade routes, nor do they follow the traditional pattern of urban growth. Only the smaller capitals of essentially rural inland countries, such as Bamako (Mali), Ouagadougou (Burkina Faso) and Niamey (Niger) have retained the traditional aspect of African multilingual communities, with a separate quarter for each major ethnic group, usually associated with distinct and often rural activities. The great urban centres of the coast owe their origin to the first European trading stations and the subsequent establishment of the colonial administration. As such they have been multilingual from the beginning, and an examination of the development of these towns will give us a better understanding of their patterns of language use and the effect this has had on the development of lingua francas.

As a result of the abolition of the slave trade in the 19th century the previous coastal forts, such as St. Louis, Goree, Bissau, Elmina and others, were transformed into legitimate trading stations, while additional coastal enclaves were founded as settlements for freed slaves, such as Freetown, Bathurst and Monrovia. All these settlements had one thing in common: they had a mixed population consisting of transient European merchants, their settled mixed-race descendants, freed African slaves as well as African merchants and labourers in European employment, to which were added Lebanese and Syrian merchants by the end of the century. This mixed population usually had no allegiance to the local African hierarchy, nor any linguistic–cultural affinities with the surrounding population, and in most cases French, English or Portuguese, or a creolised version of these languages, was used as lingua franca, if not as mother tongue. This is still the case in Freetown, Monrovia, Bissau and the Cap Verde Islands, whereas in other coastal towns a secondary linguistic influence soon made itself felt through the increase in the proportion of indigenous African town dwellers.

Towns which became the seat of the colonial administration reflected their radius of influence in an increasingly multi-ethnic and multilingual population, coming to seek employment, education and social promotion. With independence these cities became the capitals and major towns of the new African states and continued to grow at a very fast rate. And while previously only the neighbouring ethnic groups had tended to migrate to the coastal cities, there was now an increased tendency for migration in stages: from the distant marginalised rural communities to country towns and from there eventually to the capital. In addition, the initially temporary urban migration became more and more permanent, and as a consequence urban centres have become increasingly heterogeneous.

Other multilingual communities grew up around the many smaller trading posts which multiplied in the interior during the 19th century, or developed out of former slave villages established in the vicinity of military and administrative posts, villages which supplied the colonial administration with labour for construction projects and in domestic service. Such villages existed all through French West Africa and, by the beginning of the 20th century, housed approximately one quarter of the total African population, and in some areas as much as 50%. These multi-ethnic communities were the first to break with the traditional concept of close knit and clan based social units, and time seems to have worked in favour of a fusion of the various ethnic groups, since the need for a common lingua franca paved the way for language shift.[10]

The sociolinguistic development in the big coastal cities, especially the capital cities, followed along similar lines, but with the difference that their ethno-linguistic composition tends to reflect that of the country as a whole and in some cases—due to immigration from other African countries—it may be even more heterogeneous. Furthermore, it can be said that whatever lingua franca spreads in a capital city is invariably of national importance, just as the new social stratification developing in urban centres, which is based on education and skills rather than on status by birth, paves the way for a new national consciousness. As has been pointed out by many linguists and sociolinguists, there is no need to plan for or impose a lingua franca: the development of a mode of communication is an inbuilt dynamic mechanism of any human agglomeration. There is thus no urban centre which does not have a dominant, or at least preferred lingua franca, and in many cases this lingua franca becomes the native language of the majority of the second generation townspeople, irrespective of their ethnic origin. The choice of the urban lingua franca is frequently determined by the first inhabitants or the majority group of the district in which the town is situated. How long the urban immigrant is able to maintain his first language and emotional attachment to it depends on the existence of ethnic associations, ties to the village and the degree of more or less compulsory contact with members of other ethnic groups, be they local or immigrant, at work and in the market place.

The case of the urban and sociolinguistic development of Dakar, the capital of Senegal, appears to be a classical example. Founded in 1857 on the territory of a Wolof speaking clan, Dakar soon overtook St. Louis, the earliest seat of French colonial administration, because of its superior port facilities. The first immigrants to Dakar came from St. Louis and other Wolof speaking provinces in the neighbourhood of Dakar. In 1902 Dakar became the centre of colonial administration and the seat of the Governor General of all French West Africa, and as such attracted a great diversity of people. However, members of the Wolof group and their language continued to be the dominant feature of Dakar's urban life. Several surveys of language use in Dakar and other Senegalese urban centres revealed to what extent Wolof was spreading, both as lingua franca and as first language of the young generation born in town (cf. Chapter 5). There can be no doubt that this acceptance of the lingua franca and eventual language shift is essentially motivated by practical considerations, in view of the fact that settling in town may be a question of survival, not only of the individuals concerned, but often of the relatives remaining in the village and depending on the migrant's support. And while the village links tend to keep the mother tongue alive, the second generation falls increasingly under the influence of the more individualist ethics of the townspeople and is more likely to abandon the parents' mother tongue in favour of the town's lingua franca. This seems to hold true even for those who have joined the French educated élite.[11]

Other capital cities with a dominant lingua franca are: *Bamako* (Bambara, a Manding dialect), *Cotonou* (the Ewe dialect Fon), *Konakry* (Susu), *Lagos* (Yoruba), *Lome* (the Ewe dialect Mina), *Niamey* (Songhai) and *Ouagadougou* (More). In the remaining capital cities the situation of the preferred lingua franca is less well defined, essentially because the conditions which favoured the original choice have changed in the last 20 or 30 years. For instance Freetown, originally a settlement of freed slaves whose only common language was a creolised form of English (Krio), had a population composed of 50% of Creole descent at the beginning of the 1920s. However, new immigrants from the hinterland were unable to penetrate into the closely knit Creole community and with increasing urban migration since independence the two lingua francas of the hinterland (Temne and Mende) have invaded the capital.[12] A similar development seems to have taken place in Abidjan, where the highly diverse population used to communicate in a creolised version of French (called *petit francais* or *petit nègre*). However, since this variety served mainly the illiterates a growing tendency has been observed since the seventies to use Jula, the prestigious trade language and lingua franca of the northern districts of Ivory Coast. Djite (1988) claims that 85% of the inhabitants of Abidjan now prefer to use Jula for purposes of inter-ethnic communication.

In the smaller inland towns, often of precolonial origin and nowadays of secondary importance, the pattern of language use has in most cases been determined long ago and changed very little. Thus, Heine (1970) points out that in the old Sahelian trading towns Gao, Timbuktu, Jenne and Mopti (all in northern Mali) Songhai is still used as the urban lingua franca, despite the spread of Bambara (Manding) elsewhere in Mali.

The effect of modern urban migration can thus be summarised in two points:

(a) urbanisation did indeed create increased linguistic heterogeneity, for nowhere are so many languages brought into as close a contact as in the context of urban conglomerations, especially the modern African capitals on the coast;

(b) this situation of multilingual mixing bowls seems to have accelerated the process of linguistic assimilation by making the adoption of a common lingua franca a *vital necessity*. The implications of this phenomenon are of utmost importance for the future of the countries concerned, and although lingua francas are not likely to play the same role in the rural context, because there may not be the same need for, nor the same intensity of inter-ethnic contact, the lesson to be learned is the recognition that *socio-economic integration is the key to linguistic unification.* An economically marginalised ethnic minority is not likely to embrace joyfully an enforced language change.

The Sociolinguistic Inheritance of the Independent West African States

Before examining the actual sociolinguistic situation in West African countries there is one further question which needs to be answered: it concerns the forces and decisions to which these countries owe their territorial shape and ethnolinguistic composition. In the first instance, the political borders of modern African states are based on the arbitrary partition of African territories between the rival colonial powers, as agreed upon at the Berlin Conference (1884/85) and as adjusted or confirmed by further agreements and the military conquest. It is important to understand that partition occurred *before* conquest. In fact, what was agreed upon at that conference were the *spheres of influence*, by which was meant an unspecified hinterland behind the already established coastal trading forts and various *protectorates* acquired through treaties with Africans. The as yet unconquered territories of the hinterland were defined in terms of natural boundaries wherever possible, or by degrees of latitude and longitude. (cf. Uzoigwe, 1985) This small detail seems very significant for the colonialist's attitude: for all intents and purposes a colony was an empty chunk of real estate, and that it was inhabited and by whom was largely irrelevant. In some cases where little was known about the interior the importance of such territories was primarily geopolitical. However, the agreements signed in Berlin had to be confirmed by effective occupation, and it was this which launched the real scramble: the speedily organised military campaigns which aimed at obtaining as large a chunk as possible, before the rival power could get there.

One particular case may be mentioned as an example of the sometimes incongruous methods applied in the partition of African territories. Both the British and the French had established trading forts on the Gambia river, but in the 1850s Britain obtained exclusive control over the Gambia trade following a deal with France. Later, Britain attempted to make yet another deal and exchange Gambia for Gabon, which failed, and finally in 1889 the two powers came to an agreement. Here a word of explanation might be necessary: Gambia consists of a thin slice of territory of between 10 and 20 kilometres on each side of the river, surrounded by the former French colony Senegal on three sides. In order to determine the border, a British gunship went upstream as far as it could, shooting its canon every now and again. The limit of audibility of these shots became the borders between Senegal and Gambia.

For obvious reasons the division between the territories of rival colonial powers were most keenly felt; but the advantage which France had won by appropriating the largest contiguous chunk of West Africa was soon cancelled by subdivisions and rivalries between the governors of each of the French colonies, and by the final shape these colonies took after a number of re-shuffles. By 1920 the original five colonies of the 1890s—Senegal, Guinea, Ivory Coast, Dahomey and Sudan, were rearranged into seven colonies, to which later Mauritania and Togo were added to make up the nine members of the AOF (French West Africa). Most of these final subdivisions created borders as incongruous as those between rival colonial powers. The old French Sudan lost some of its savanna areas to Ivory Coast and Guinea, thus subdividing the linguistically homogeneous core of Manding territories between Mali, Ivory Coast and Guinea, while its eastern regions became Upper Volta (now Burkina Faso) with a Manding speaking minority, and Niger, which created further ethnolinguistic divisions.

It was these borders, established in the manners described above, which were recognised by the heads of state of the newly independent African countries when they signed the charter of the *Organisation of African Unity* in 1963, which pledges as one of its principles to 'respect the sovereignty and territorial integrity of each state'. This then was the final step in a series of power struggles and negotiations which determined the ethnolinguistic composition of modern African states.

In order to demonstrate what this means in sociolinguistic terms I refer to Table 1, which lists a selection of major languages in West Africa whose native speakers' communities are divided between two or more countries. The main purpose of this table is to demonstrate the extent to which linguistic heterogeneity in West Africa is the result of the fact that political borders do not coincide with linguistic boundaries. While it is a valid argument that in the case of many ethnolinguistic groups a territorial limitation would be almost impossible now, because of frequent overlapping and because of the population movements described above, it must be evident that at an early stage more or less homogeneous territories could have been outlined, particularly if they fell within the jurisdiction of one colonial power.

Two languages in Table 1 are particularly striking because of the magnitude of their geographical extension: Manding and Pulaar; while others are essentially split up between two or three countries. The case of Manding spread has already been dealt with in Chapter 2, but this table relates language spread to demographic factors. Furthermore, it shows that the bulk of Manding speakers live in six of the former French colonies, and that with the exception of Gambia and Guinea Bissau these included all the traditional Manding territories.

The case of Pulaar is somewhat different. This language, spoken by the Fulbe, Fulani and Tukulor communities, owes its expansion to the fact that its native speakers were nomadic or semi-nomadic herdsmen, living and moving among the agricultural communities of other ethnic groups, but maintaining their ethnolinguistic and cultural identity. Their settlement occurred mainly during the last four centuries and their various state formations in the course of their precolonial history were independent of one another and their language considerably fragmented. In the context of

Table 1 West African languages across borders[13]

	Pulaar	Manding	Soninka	Songhai	Wolof	Hausa	Kanuri	Yoruba	Sena	Eve-Fon
MAURITANIA Pop 1.946m	6.0% *(117)	1.0% (19)	3.0% (58)		7.0% (136)					
SENEGAL Pop 6.1614m	21.0% (1,389)	5.7% (377)	1.8% (119)		44.1% (2,910)					
MALI Pop 8.438m	14.0% (1,181)	38.0% (3,206)	9.0% (759)	6.4% (540)					9.2% (776)	
GAMBIA Pop 0.656m	18.0% (118)	42.0% (276)	8.7% (57)		16.0% (105)					
GUINEA BISSAU Pop 0.906m	23.0% (208)	12.0% (109)								
GUINEA Pop 6.225m	40.0% (2,490)	22.0% (1,369)								
SIERRA LEONE Pop 3.670m	3.1% (114)	2.3% (84)								
LIBERIA Pop 2.221m		7.2% (160)								
IVORY COAST Pop 10.165m		11.0% (1,118)							10.0% (1,016)	
BURKINA FASO Pop 6.745m	ND	6.9% (466)		ND					5.5% (371)	
GHANA Pop 14.045m						ND			ND	13.0% (1,826)
TOGO Pop 3.052m								ND		27.9% (851)
BENIN Pop 4.042m	2.4% (97)			2.1% (85)		ND		14.0% (566)		56.6% (2,288)
NIGER Pop 6.298m	14.0% (882)			21.0% (1,323)		46.0% (2,897)	7.6% (479)			
NIGERIA Pop 98.517m	8.6% (8,472)			ND		21.0% (20,689)	4.1% (4,039)	20.0% (19,703)		ND
TOTAL OF NATIVE SPEAKERS	15.068m	7.184m	0.993m	1.948m	3.151m	23.586m	4.518m	20.269m	2.163m	4.965m

* estimates of native speakers in thousands
ND = no data available

the modern West African states their linguistic influence is small and limited to the areas where their native speakers are concentrated, such as northern Senegal, and the central highlands of Guinea and Guinea Bissau. Despite their numerical strength in Nigeria, the local dialect *Fulani* is spoken only as a mother tongue and most of the Fulani speakers use Hausa as a lingua franca. The language has also spread beyond West Africa, into Cameroon and Chad.

Hausa and Yoruba, having the biggest native speaker communities, were less severely affected by colonial partitions because in each case a viable community exists in each of the two countries where they are concentrated. Inevitably, the smaller the number of speakers, the more serious were the consequences of sub-division and fragmentation of such languages, particularly in terms of the role such languages might play internally. Soninka is a case in point: linguists claim that despite registration under this ethnic label, Soninka is no longer spoken in the Gambia. In Senegal it figures on the list of six national languages, but its speakers are completely scattered, most of them working as immigrant labourers in France, and in Mali and Mauritania the situation is not much different. A list of smaller language communities fragmented by borders would take up many pages and the smallest of them owe their near-extinction partly to this problem.

On the other hand, in a hypothetical country based on larger linguistic affinities, increased contact is likely to create a tendency towards convergence, and in such a context a forceful programme of studies in dialectology would sooner or later be able to contribute to some form of linguistic unification. By larger linguistic affinities I mean languages which consist of a dialect continuum which, when interrupted by state borders, become irrevocably fragmented into isolated languages. This case is illustrated by the last language on Table 1, identified as *Eve-Fon*. Mann & Dalby (1987) list this as one dialect cluster, although now there is little inter-comprehension between the individual dialects. Eve (or Evebe) has its main native speakers' communities in south-eastern Ghana and Togo and was standardised by protestant missionaries at an early stage. Further to the east catholic missionaries concentrated their effort on the dialect *Mina* (Genbe) while the dialects *Fon* (Fonbe) and *Ajabe* of Benin were considered to be too distant and, probably because of this exclusion, became more isolated and fragmented.

A similar situation is presented in Map 4, according to which Ivory Coast is neatly divided into five sections: the Manding speaking northwest, a continuation of the Manding territories of Mali and Guinea; the area of southern Mande languages which continues into Liberia and Sierra Leone;

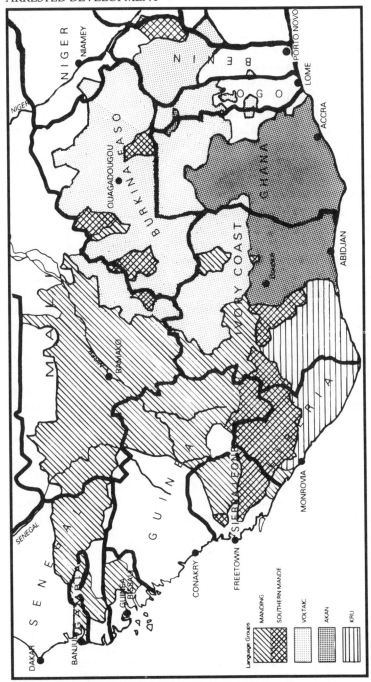

Map 4 Larger linguistic groups in West Africa

the area of Kru (West Atlantic) languages which also continue into Liberia; the Voltaic languages of the northeast which stretch into Burkina Faso and northern Ghana; and lastly the southeast with its Akan languages extending over two thirds of Ghana. In the latter group there are the dialects Anyi-Bawule, spoken by 30.4% of the population of Ivory Coast and Twi-Fante spoken by 42.7% of the population of Ghana, altogether a population of nearly 10 million. These related ethnolinguistic groups still had intensive contacts until the last century and, at some stage, the Ashanti kings ruled over the western (Ivory Coast) provinces. In fact the western provinces became a popular escape route in the last stages of the Ashanti struggle with the British colonial army. In Mann & Dalby (1987) these are listed as belonging to the same inter-intelligible dialect cluster.

To conclude this chapter: the developments which took place in West Africa in the last four to five centuries had a very significant impact on the present sociolinguistic situation in the fifteen independent countries. In the first instance, the first trading contacts between European nations and West African coastal societies were one of the reasons for the decline of the Mali empire and the arrest of the linguistic unification process started in its heyday. Secondly, as this trade developed into three centuries of trans-Atlantic slave trade, the linguistic fragmentation of the coastal belt and its immediate hinterland continued to be aggravated. Subsequently, forced or voluntary labour migration and rapid urbanisation created multilingual mixing bowls, in which traditional bonds and linguistic loyalties fell victim to the need to adapt and survive. Lastly, the partition of West Africa into fifteen colonies resulted in increased linguistic fragmentation , because so many ethnolinguistic groups were divided into two or more parts by the colonial and later state borders. From the point of view of social and linguistic development this can only be described as a regression from the previous situation, even in the so-called 'stateless' societies. It therefore needs to be stressed that linguistic heterogeneity in African countries, as it exists today, is neither a natural condition nor is it an inevitable feature of the African sociolinguistic make-up, but the logical result of the colonial conquest and all the events which led up to it. This insight will help us understand the current situation to which our attention will be turned in the following chapter.

Notes to Chapter 4

1. Among others there are the apologists of imperialism who want to belittle the effects of the slave trade. Fage (1969), for instance, argues that the export of slaves from West Africa only slightly exceeded natural population growth in the 18th century, and was lower in the previous centuries, and that in the more densely populated areas ...'it may have been more profitable (!) /.../ to have

exported the equivalent of its natural growth of population rather than to have kept it at home' (p.89). He also speaks about the *value* of the goods offered in return for slaves, when these were in the majority guns, spirits and beads.

2. cf. Rodney (1975: 290).

3. In Senegal these consist of about 5000 Basari and an estimated 2000 others belonging to two or three smaller sub-groups of the Tenda (cf. Mansour, 1980). In all these cases the border between Senegal and Guinea separates these communities from the more substantial communities of their ethnic brothers in Guinea.

4. This is particularly noticeable since the establishment of a Christian mission teaching the villagers useful skills which subsequently help them to find work in the neighbouring towns (cf. Nolan, 1977).

5. The two major languages of assimilation in this part of West Africa were Manding and Pulaar. Thus, according to Roche (1976), the social group called *Fula-dion* in Upper Casamance, who speak a dialect of Pulaar, had adopted their masters' language and became assimilated.

6. These two became heros whose fame continues to move popular imagination and their influence can still be felt today. For the Manding the hero was *Samori Toure*, son of a Muslim Jula, who started as chief of his mother's pagan warrior clan. By 1873 he had become the master of the linguistically homogeneous Manding territories from the southern forest limits (Sierra Leone and Liberia) to Bamako, and from the Futa Jallon to Sikasso. After mounting pressure from the French colonial army he moved east into Ivory Coast where his new empire extended all along the forest fringe into Ghana, where he was finally cornered between the French and British armies in 1898 and captured. The other hero, *Al Hajj Omar Tall*, a Tukulor and head of the Tijaniyya Muslim brotherhood, started his empire building in 1850 in the eastern part of the Futa Jallon. Eventually his power spread north, along the Senegal river to Kaarta, Segu, Masina and the Niger bend. He was killed in battle in 1864 and his heirs were defeated by the French between 1888 and 1893. (For more details cf. among others, M'Baye Gueye & Boahen (1985)).

7. cf. Suret-Canale (1973: Vol.2) concerning the methods employed by the French in their conquest which proceeded from the mouth of the Senegal river in the middle of the 19th century. Firstly, the rivalries for succession to the leadership of one of the Wolof kingdoms was used to establish a puppet ruler, who then proceeded to attack other Wolof chiefdoms. Wolof pressure was then used against the Tukulor ruler further up the Senegal river, who in turn helped the French to stop the advance of his rival Omar Tall. Likewise, in the advance on the Niger thirty years later, friendship treaties with the two powerful rulers (Samori and Omar Tall) were used against the lesser chiefs, but once military posts had been established on the Niger, the French incited the local population to revolt against their rulers. Despite different appearances, similar methods were employed by the British. On the Gold Coast, for instance, a military alliance with the coastal Fante federation was directed against the Ashanti kingdom of the interior. In Lagos, the British gained their first foothold by supporting and then installing a rival king, who in return facilitated the establishment of British trading companies. The Yoruba resistance to annexation to the Protectorate of

Southern Nigeria was finally squashed by exploiting internal hostilities between the various Yoruba kingdoms.

8. cf. Crowder (1968) and Amin (1974).

9. For instance, the rubber tappers working for British companies in the Gambia were *Aku* from Sierra Leone, who had originally come from the Lagos area and were at least partly of Yoruba descent, speaking Krio. They became the urban middle class, holding high positions in the administration and commerce and were resented by the local population. In Senegalese Casamance there are two substantial immigrant groups from the Bissau area: the Manjaku rubber tappers who settled in the vicinity of Ziguinchor (about 23,000 inhabitants) and their rice cultivating cousins the Mankana, thus adding two more languages to an already highly multilingual district.

10. For instance, the town Sedhiou in the Casamance district of Senegal was originally a fortified trading station established in 1837. By 1857 its African population had risen to 770 inhabitants from seven different ethnic groups, among them Manding and Wolof (cf. Roche, 1976). Due to the assimilation process Sedhiou is now dominated by Manding speakers (67% of the population according to the 1976 census), with Wolof speakers forming the second largest component (20%).

11. A sociolinguistic investigation into the use of French (Blonde, 1975) accidentally throws some light onto the use of Wolof by the francophone élite of Dakar, and the social reasons for their linguistic behaviour. In the domains of family and friendship, the market place and the street, Wolof emerges as by far the most frequently spoken language, even though only 50% of the sample were native speakers of Wolof. When asked to rank languages in order of importance, 53% of these subjects ranked French as indispensable and 33% as very useful in their professional life; nevertheless 35% *ranked Wolof as the most important language*, compared to 44% giving the first position to French.

12. cf. Tabouret-Keller (1971) who further mentions the interesting example of the Ghanaian capital Accra. The original inhabitants of Accra were speakers of Ga, and although they make up only about 3.5% of the Ghanaian population, their language had received a lot of attention from German missionaries in the 19th century, who transcribed and used this language in education. During its early stage Ga was the lingua franca of Accra. However, in the rest of Ghana the most important language is Twi, spoken by about 60% of the population total and, consequently, immigrating Twi speakers soon formed the largest component of Accra's population and their language took hold of the capital.

13. This table is based on the information published in Mann & Dalby (1987) and, in the case of Manding spoken in Liberia, I refer to Gnielinski (1972). The population statistics have been taken from the *United Nations Demographic Yearbook 1986* and represent estimates of the mid-year population of 1986 (in thousands). The percentages on the table refer to the percentage of the total population of a given country, speaking the listed language as mother tongue. The figures below refer to the estimates (in thousands) of the total mother tongue community of the listed language.

5 Multilingualism and Social Transition in Contemporary West Africa

Although the degree of linguistic heterogeneity varies considerably from one West African country to another, they are all multilingual and language use is determined by the functional roles of the languages in any one country. This means that some indigenous languages are used purely for communication within the ethnic group (in-group languages), while others are also used for inter-ethnic communication (lingua francas) and one of the languages of the previous colonial powers has the status of official language.

However, this actual state of affairs is very rarely given official recognition, and that for a variety of reasons. In the first instance, as we have seen in Chapter 1, linguistic and anthropological studies in Africa tended to ignore the functions and social roles of languages within a larger socio-political context and concentrated on establishing a catalogue of African vernaculars instead. That these vernaculars ranged from dialects spoken by small splinter groups on the one hand to languages spoken by communities of 10 or 20 million on the other, was not taken into consideration. Furthermore, the criteria used to label languages and group people into ethnic or 'tribal' groups were undefined and often questionable. However, sociolinguistic research has made some advance, and the following sub-section is an attempt at providing a brief over-view of the sociolinguistic situation, based on the principles discussed in Chapter 1 (page 16).

A Sociolinguistic Profile of West African Countries

The data presented in Table 2 is based on Mann & Dalby (1987) and comes from a variety of sources, but the estimates concerning lingua franca speakers are likely to be conservative. In some countries language surveys were carried out in order to determine the spread of a given lingua franca, but it seems that such surveys frequently touched upon sensitive political issues and were either prevented, or had their findings distorted and

Table 2 Functional profile of languages in West Africa

	Majority Language	Sub-National Lingua Francas	Their Area of Influence	Minority Languages and their Status	Special Status /Official Language
BENIN	none	Fon 57% T? Yoruba 15% T? Hausa LF	south east north	4 National L/s + 7 undefined	French
BURKINA FASO	Moore 48%> T60%	Manding/Jula 7%> T10%	west	11 National L/s + 7 undefined	French
GAMBIA	Manding 42%> T60%	Wolof 16% T?	capital	4 undefined	English
GHANA	Twi-Fante 40%> T60%	Eve 13% T? Hausa LF	south-east north	7 Education L/s + 10 undefined	English
GUINEA	none	Pulaar 40% T? Manding 22% T? Susu 10%> T20%	central plat. north-east capital, coast	5 National L/s + 6 undefined	French
GUINEA BISSAU	Kriol (cf. note 2)	none		14 undefined	Portuguese
IVORY COAST	none	Manding/Jula 11%> T61% Anyi/Bawule 30%> T64% Pidgin French LF	north, urban south/rural south/urban	2 Education L/s + 16 undefined	French
LIBERIA	none	Manding/Vai T33% Kru-English LF		10 undefined	English
MALI	Manding 38%> T80%	Songhai 7%> T15%	north	6 National L/s + 4 undefined	French
MAURITANIA	Arabic 80% T?	none		4 undefined	French & Arabic
NIGER	Hausa 46%> T85%	Songhai 21% T?	west	3 National L/s + 2 undefined	French
NIGERIA	none	Hausa 21%> T38% Yoruba 20%> T25% Ibo 17%> T22%	north south-west south-east	9 State L/s + 61 undefined	English
SENEGAL	Wolof 44%> T80%	Pulaar 21% T? Manding 6% T?	north-east south-east	6 National L/s + 7 undefined	French
SIERRA LEONE	none	Mende 34%> T43% Temne 30%> T32% Krio 2% T?	south north urban	6 undefined	English
TOGO	none	Eve 22%> T48% Kabye 13%> T32%	south north	14 undefined	French

Key: first figure = native speakers (% of national population)
T = estimate of total (native speakers plus lingua franca speakers as % of pop.)
T? = no estimates available
LF = lingua franca speakers only

possibly suppressed. For instance, a certain UNESCO survey[1] was handicapped by the fact that the educational or cultural authorities of many member countries did not complete the questionnaire that was sent to them, while others appear to have misinterpreted the term 'community languages' and instead gave information concerning their 'national languages'. The latter term defines the status of a language, but not necessarily its functional role, whereas the survey defined *community language* as 'a language which is the dominant and general means of communication in a district, province or similar larger area' (including cities) and contrasted it with 'family languages', otherwise also called *mother tongues*. In other words, what was required was information concerning lingua francas. This term is preferable because it seems less ambiguous than the term *community language*, as used by UNESCO. At the same time I should add that if a lingua franca is to develop into a future national language, it must also be a 'community language', namely home-grown, with a local mother tongue community with which other ethnic groups of the country have been in contact and with which they can identify because of the shared social and cultural characteristics. For this reason I exclude foreign languages from this category, although at the international level these are in fact 'lingua francas'.

The main purpose of Table 2 is to give an overall impression of the functional roles of the indigenous languages in these countries and to serve as a basis for comparison as to the degree and type of multilingualism prevalent in them. As outlined in Chapter 1 there are four main functional categories: majority language (or major lingua franca), sub-national lingua francas, minority languages and special status languages. The second category is useful and, indeed, essential in order to distinguish between situations where a major, national lingua franca exists and those where the lingua francas have only a limited radius of influence (usually described in geographical terms, such as 'north', 'south', etc.) The third category contains the bulk of African languages which are used only for *communication within the ethnic group* (the mother tongues or family languages), many of which also happen to be small in size and hence *minority languages*. In this category one may find languages which were singled out by the respective governments and were either given the status of a *national language* or allotted a limited function in education. In contrast to these there are languages which do not have any official status or function, but are listed in Mann & Dalby's *Thesaurus of African Languages*. Since a profile cannot list all minority languages, Table 2 only refers to the number of languages in this category. According to Dalby's classification system only the dialect clusters (sets) were counted. (In the case of Nigeria, for instance,

Dalby refers to 61 sets, whereas other sources mention 380 languages or more.)

Lastly, the fourth category: Special Status Languages refers mainly to foreign official languages which are at the same time the major languages of education. In countries with a Muslim population Arabic plays a certain role as the language of religion, but information concerning the actual use of Arabic is usually not available.

Of the fifteen countries listed in Table 2 Mauritania stands out as the only country which has proclaimed and is using its majority language and national lingua franca (Arabic) as official language, a position it shares with French. Three other countries—Mali, Niger and Senegal—have a local lingua franca which is spoken by 80% or more of the population and is in the process of gaining the entire country; and this without any government interference and without any special status being granted to those languages. Furthermore the estimates of lingua franca speakers are likely to be conservative since, once a language community has reached this size, its spread accelerates. In countries where 45% of the population are under fifteen years of age and where urban migration continues to grow at a fast rate, the rate of language shift can likewise be expected to accelerate.

Then there are three countries: Burkina Faso, Gambia and Ghana, where the dominant language is spoken by about 60% of the population and where rival lingua francas have a relatively small number of speakers in a geographically limited area. Though Benin, with 57% native speakers of the Fon dialect cluster comes near to this, and though the standardisation and unification of these dialects has been proposed and seems linguistically feasible, there is as yet no evidence of any progress.

The remaining countries have two or three lingua francas which, each in its area of influence as indicated, serve as vehicles for inter-ethnic communication. In Nigeria this is recognised officially through status definition which differentiates between *national* and *state languages*. Togo has likewise officially declared that its two lingua francas are considered to be national languages, each with its zone of influence, which eventually are expected to replace French in primary school education. In Guinea and Sierra Leone a similar system of complementary sub-national lingua francas is operative, though not officially sanctioned. Recent studies carried out in Ivory Coast suggest that Jula is now being preferred in interethnic communication (by about 85% of the population of Abidjan) and that it is gaining influence throughout the country.[4]

Finally there are three countries which, due to particular historical circumstances, have a long established Creole language which in the past was their major lingua franca: Guinea Bissau, Sierra Leone and Liberia.

However, recent developments in these countries show a pronounced change in the role and status of Creole languages. In the urban centres and the rural coastal areas of Liberia a Creole variant known as *Kru-English* is used as the main lingua franca, but in the northern half of the hinterland one or two varieties of Manding (Vai and Mandingo) seem to fulfil this function,[5] while the south is inhabited by Kru speakers whose dialects are largely inter- intelligible. In Sierra Leone the position of Krio also seems to be challenged by two languages of the interior: Mende and Temne, which are gaining importance as lingua francas, and are likely to replace Krio. Only in Guinea Bissau the political leadership, which formed a close alliance with the Cap Verde Islands since the early 1980s, favours the promotion of Kriol as the future national language, but no definite steps seem to have been taken in that direction.

From the brief outline given above it emerges that the sociolinguistic profile of modern African countries is influenced by two factors: (a) the spontaneous, internal sociolinguistic development which results in a division of labour between lingua francas and languages which serve only in-group communication, and (b) the government's language policy. In the context of newly independent countries language policy and language planning have been considered important tools of nation building and therefore deserve to be given more attention.

Language Policy: Before and After Independence

The legacy of the colonial language policy is so all-pervading that it affected , or in some cases paralysed any subsequent policy decisions. Any examination of language policy therefore has to begin with the policy of the colonial administration.

One of the tasks confronting colonial administrators was to devise an educational system which would provide them with the necessary manpower to fill the lower ranks in colonial government and commercial establishments. In some parts of Africa administrators were influenced by Protestant missionaries who had always acted upon the principle of preaching the gospel in the native language of those whom they wished to convert. The ground work in linguistic studies and basic education thus having been done by the missionaries, the Belgian, German and British administrators had a core of literate Africans at their disposal, which facilitated what the British called 'indirect rule'. Henceforth a number of African languages played an important role in primary education and communication at the local level. This policy contrasted considerably with the French and Portuguese policies, which resulted in the exclusive use of

French and Portuguese in their colonies, and a ban on the use of local languages in education.

These two different approaches had as their major consequence the scientific advance of a certain number of African languages over others. In West Africa these were Hausa, Yoruba, Ibo, Twi, Ga and Eve, which at the time of independence had up to 80 years of linguistic studies, literacy work and practical application in the modern sector behind them, while basic studies had barely begun in the former French colonies, and not at all in those of the Portuguese. The francophone and lusophone African countries (with the exception of Mauritania) were therefore in no position to make any change in language policy.

In theory at least, the anglophone countries had a choice, though in practice the difference did not turn out to be all that great. When it came to deciding on an official language, all the anglophone independent countries in West Africa elected to keep English as the sole official language. However, in the domain of education the new language policy differed considerably from that of the former French and Portuguese colonies; it also differed from one country to another. Yet, the ultimate goal of education appears to be the same in most of the countries included in this study: mastery of the European official language is considered to be the only road to personal economic and social advance and, ostensibly, the only hope for development and modernisation for the country as a whole. Furthermore, in some particularly heterogeneous countries the official language has been proclaimed as the language of 'national unity'. Consequently a number of changes were made in the educational policy of Nigeria and Ghana which, in the name of national unity, in fact reduced the extent to which African languages were used.[6]

In most countries the process of selection and status definition of indigenous languages has begun, as witnessed by the references to 'national languages' in Table 2. However, it is difficult to assess what exactly the future role of these languages is supposed to be, other than that of being introduced in the initial stages of education. But the fact that a certain number of languages are excluded from the list of national languages implies that the excluded languages are considered to be marginal. On the other hand, the criteria for exclusion or inclusion are never formulated and, judging by demographic data, seem to be haphazard.[7] Furthermore, there are still a number of countries which have made no statements concerning the status of any of their local languages.

Thanks to the efforts of UNESCO, education in the mother tongue has become accepted in principle and now figures in all the policy statements of African heads of state and ministers of education. Nevertheless, the implementation of such policies varies greatly, as can be assessed from Table 3 which lists the languages used in education, and mentions whether they are used as medium of education or merely as a subject, and at what level.

Five of the listed countries have as yet not been able to solve any of the problems related to mother tongue education and are still following the colonial pattern of education with the exclusive use of the official language. They are Benin, Gambia, Guinea Bissau, Liberia and Sierra Leone. Of these Benin has projected the use of its national languages in primary education in the near future.

Burkina Faso has advanced one step further: two of its national languages are taught as curriculum subjects at the tertiary level (at Teachers' College) in view of their future use at primary school. In Senegal Wolof has been used progressively throughout the 1980s, while the other five national languages were still at the preparatory stage when the survey was made. The same applies to Niger, which was at that stage using its five national languages on an experimental basis.

The remaining countries have established a pattern of initial mother tongue education, for phases of varying length, with the mother tongue used as medium of education and the official language gradually replacing it by the end of primary school or in secondary school. In many cases the major languages are also offered as curriculum subjects in secondary and/or at the tertiary level, a system which aims at teaching these particular languages to speakers of other languages.

However praiseworthy the principle of mother tongue education may be from the pedagogical point of view, it is one of those concepts which have been taken over from the developed world, without any consideration for the social and economic condition of underdeveloped countries; and most certainly without any concern for the task of nation-building which now confronts these countries. In fact there is a danger that such educational policies could increase, or permanently rigidify linguistic heterogeneity. The strict application of the principle of mother tongue education could arrest the natural process of language shift away from minority languages to the lingua franca of the district or country. Particularly in urban centres with their highly diverse ethnic composition the implementation of such a policy would appear to be extremely complex and costly. Furthermore the promise of mother tongue education is only likely to confuse parents and lead them to reject something which under another label they might accept. In practice urban schools should employ the dominant lingua franca which tends to be spoken by children and adults alike (cf. next section).

Table 3 Languages used in government education

	Primary Education Medium of Instr.	Secondary Education Medium/Subject	Tertiary Education Medium/Subject
BENIN	French	French M/S	French M/S
BURKINA FASO	French	French M/S	French M/S Moore S, Manding S
GAMBIA	English	English M/S	English M/S
GHANA	English Twi, Eve, Gan/Danme Dagara/Dabane, Nzema Kasem, Abanito	English M/S Twi M/S, Eve M/S Gan/Danme M/S	English M/S Twi S, Eve S
GUINEA	French Pulaar, Manding, Susu, Kisiel, Basari Loma/Peleewo	French M/S Pulaar S, Manding S Susu S, Kisiel S, Loma S, Basari S	French Pulaar S, Manding S Susu S, Kisiel S, Loma S, Basari S
GUINEA BISSAU	Portuguese	Portuguese M/S	Portuguese M/S
IVORY COAST	French Bawule, Manding, Sena, Dan	French M/S	French M/S Bawule S, Manding S Sena S, Bete S
LIBERIA	English	English M/S	English M/S
MALI	French Manding Pulaar	French M/S	- - -
MAURITANIA	French, Arabic	French, Arabic M/S	- - -
NIGER	French Experimental: Hausa	French M/S	- - -
NIGERIA	English Hausa, Yoruba, Ibo, Kanuri, Ibibo-Efik, Edo/Bini, Pulaar, Tiv, Ejo, Nupe, Igala, Idoma (plus many other languages used for initial year or two)	English M/S Hausa S, Yoruba S Ibo S, Kanuri S, Ibibo-Efik S	English M/S Hausa S, Yoruba S, Ibo S, Kanuri S, Edo-Bini s
SENEGAL	French Wolof	French M/S	French M/S
SIERRA LEONE	English	English M/S	English M/S
TOGO	French Eve, Kabye	French M/S Eve S, Kabye S	French M/S

(based on Mann & Dalby, 1987)

There have been several attempts at shifting the emphasis to the useful-ness of lingua francas[8] but no deliberate recommendation has been made to revise the policy of mother tongue education. One can only conclude that the experts' insistence on the pedagogical value of mother tongue education is providing the present African élite with a very subtle escape route: while following the advice of international experts, they may quietly shelve the issue until such time as more funds are available for research and development of the local languages. For the moment at least, this has silenced the demands for the rehabilitation of African languages; and imperceptibly their role has been reduced to that of a nursery maid, who gently introduces the African child to the world of adults—a world which now as ever is dominated by a non-African language. Yet while policy makers studiously avoid giving the dominant lingua francas a greater role in public life, these are making a steady advance and are gaining in importance. Whatever language policy African governments might es-pouse in the future, the most hopeful room for manoeuvre and the most suitable recipient for language planning would seem to be the lingua francas.

The Growing Importance of Lingua Francas

Lingua francas have existed ever since and wherever different ethno-linguistic groups have come into contact. We have seen in Chapter 2 how Manding, an important lingua franca in West Africa since the Middle Ages, expanded in the context of long distance trade and the expanding Mali empire. Despite the fact that most of the favourable conditions contributing to the dominant position of Manding had disappeared with the collapse of the empire, its importance as a lingua franca continued into modern times. By the end of the 19th century the Manding dialect Jula had gained new territories in addition to the provinces that had formed part of the Mali empire and were traditionally Manding speaking territories. One of the witnesses of this development on the eve of the colonial conquest was Binger, a French traveller, who comments in 1892 that anyone speaking Jula had no trouble making himself understood anywhere in the West Volta region (now Burkina Faso).[9] Manding continued to spread as a lingua franca in the various colonies, as did the process of language shift to Jula, or any other Manding dialect. One particular instrument in the spread of Manding (Bambara) was the French colonial army, which appar-ently recruited many of its soldiers from this warlike people until Bambara became the lingua franca of the colonial army in all of French West Africa.

The main African lingua francas have attracted considerable scholarly attention[10], and yet there still persists a certain amount of confusion as to what is and what is not a lingua franca. Particularly in popular parlance lingua francas are frequently understood to mean 'trade language' or 'market language', for trade is the most common contact situation and hence the most frequent domain for lingua francas. This has led to a tendency to equate lingua francas with *pidgins* and *creoles*, hybrid languages which developed in African coastal trade between Europeans and Africans.

As Table 2 shows, such languages gained importance in some West African countries, however, the conditions under which they developed and spread have changed considerably. The creole population is no longer in the majority, nor is their socio-economic position privileged, as it was during the colonial period. Hence, the position of the creole languages are no longer at an advantage in relation to the local lingua francas; on the contrary, they may even have a certain social handicap because they are a reminder of the colonial period. Furthermore they are by no means 'neutral', in the sense that some trade languages are neutral by virtue of being outside the local power struggle. Since creole languages tend to be associated with a previously privileged group, part of the anti-colonial spirit has affected the prestige and status of these languages, and other lingua francas are now replacing the creoles.[11]

The interpretation which limits the function of lingua francas to trade contacts, such as those 'market languages' studied by Calvet (1987) in the markets of China, Congo-Brazzaville and Niger, likewise takes too narrow a definition of this term. The very fact that market languages can vary with the type of goods or from one market to the other in the same town reveals the limitations of market languages and of the concept as such.

While one should not underestimate the importance of trade for the spread of lingua francas, trade contacts are too narrow and too limited in their function to have a lasting impact on social relations in general. In the sense that I have been using the term lingua franca: as major languages for inter-ethnic communication (national or sub-national lingua francas), they have multiple social functions and hence, multiple social forces are responsible for the expansion of such languages. Their mere existence is evidence that the populations voluntarily adopting such lingua francas are to some degree aware of the need for social integration. Lingua francas are therefore the means by which multilingual countries can and do create a sense of national identity.

In those West African countries where a unique lingua franca has developed and has come to dominate most domains of social inter-action, the major contributing factors to language spread are economic development and social change. Both these factors are concentrated in the urban centres, but almost absent in distant rural districts. The latter therefore tend to be least affected by a spreading lingua franca. The role of urban development in the spread of lingua francas can be demonstrated with the case of Senegal.

As indicated in Table 2, Senegal's major lingua franca, Wolof, is spoken by 44% of the population as native language, but more than 80% of the population speak this language when second language speakers are included. In the capital, Dakar, the total of Wolof speakers amounts to approximately 96% (Wioland, 1965). An earlier survey had shown that even among the biggest and most cohesive immigrant group in Dakar (the Tukulor, who made up about 42% of Dakar's immigrants) 96% of the adults spoke Wolof. Some of the reasons why Wolof became the preferred lingua franca of the capital have already been touched upon in Chapter 4, but it is very instructive to look at the process which led to a consolidation of this tendency.

As urbanisation continued to accelerate other towns developed and received part of the flow of immigrants from the impoverished rural areas. These too adopted Wolof as lingua franca, and the trend is particularly striking in country towns far removed from the centre of the Wolof population.[12] From the previously mentioned study (Wioland, 1965) we can, in addition, obtain details concerning the process of language spread. Wioland had made a survey of languages spoken by newly enrolled primary school children in all government schools, which revealed that Wolof was not only the preferred lingua franca, but that it was gaining *as a first language* in the urban context. Children who spoke Wolof as first language (the researchers deliberately avoided the term *mother tongue* because of its ambiguity and asked for the first language spoken at home) were grouped according to the ethnic group of their father and mother. The results showed that Wolof was not only the home language in mixed marriages in which one of the parents was Wolof, but also in cases where neither parent was Wolof. In Dakar (the capital) one third of the children who were native speakers of Wolof belonged to the group of mixed marriages, as compared to two thirds which had both parents of Wolof origin. The relationship between these two types of groups was even more striking in some country towns, in one of which almost three quarters of the native speakers were children of mixed marriages as against one quarter with two Wolof parents.[13] Similar surveys in other African towns show that language shift away from minority languages, in favour of an urban lingua franca has become a common phenomenon.

The relationship between economic development and the spread of lingua francas, or their restriction to certain sub-national units, can further be substantiated by taking a closer look at those countries in West Africa in which rival lingua francas co-exist. These are invariably characterised by a particularly unequal pattern of economic development. For instance, in Ghana, Ivory Coast, Togo and Benin the southern provinces are more developed, partly because of their proximity to the coast, partly because cash crops were introduced there which were, and still are, in high demand on European markets; whereas the northern provinces in these countries have remained economically underdeveloped and rely more on traditional economic activities. They tend to be more heterogeneous, resist the spread of the southern lingua francas and use a traditional non-indigenous lingua franca, such as Hausa in Ghana and Benin. This split may also be linked to cultural factors: the Southerners were largely converted to Christianity, whereas the Northerners in all these countries tend to be Muslim.

The spread of lingua francas is very much a phenomenon of oral communication, as many studies conducted on the patterns of language choice in multilingual communities reveal. What is more, studies at the micro level as well as at the macro level show that in each case a viable system of communication evolved without any interference from a governing body or indeed any conscious effort. I shall now attempt to describe in very general terms the characteristics of such a pattern of oral communication and relate it to the modern requirements of education and literacy.

Oral Communication, Education and Literacy in the Multilingual Context

Communication needs vary according to the social and ethnic composition and the type of interaction required in each community, and the question of language choice is invariably determined by a social process akin to the social division of labour. Hence, most of the languages listed in Table 2 (particularly those listed as *Minority Languages* are used only for communication within the same ethnic group, while only a few became lingua francas used in communication with other ethnic groups. This means in actual fact that, in contrast with the latter, languages of the 'in-group' type may be restricted in their use to the domains of family and friendship, particularly in the multilingual urban context. As a consequence such languages, *because of their limited functional role,* are more likely to be affected by the coexistence with a language which has a wider functional range, and are more susceptible to language shift. On the other hand, on their home turf, in monolingual villages or wherever the speakers of such languages are sufficiently concentrated, such languages can serve most of the important domains of social interaction and are therefore not in danger of extinction.

However, in most multilingual countries situations arise where individuals from one ethnic group have to be able to communicate with individuals of another ethnic group: at the market, at work, at school and in the streets, in bars and housing estates. What makes people accept one specific language for such inter-ethnic communication, rather than another, depends on the specific social context.

It is important to stress here that the two types of languages: in-group (or family) languages and lingua francas are *complementary* and together are capable of fulfilling all the needs of communication in 'the primary domain cluster', that is to say all the basic social functions of language in a traditional oral society.[14] It was only with the attainment of statehood in the modern western sense that a written language was needed, a language which could serve in the secondary domain cluster, namely in administration, government, education, the media, etc. The language considered appropriate for these functions, the official language, was in most cases superimposed on the already existing bilingual or trilingual pattern of communication. And in most cases the official languages chosen by West African countries (cf. Table 2) are non-indigenous languages: French, English or Portuguese.

Such non-indigenous official languages differ from in-group languages and lingua francas in two important ways: the manner of acquisition and their specialised functional roles. Unlike in-group languages which are learned as first language in the home, or as second language through intense every-day contacts, and lingua francas which are usually acquired as second or further language, but also learned informally, official languages can only be acquired formally, at school or in adult literacy classes, or else they become pidginised. Their acquisition requires a deliberate and prolonged effort and is inevitably linked to literacy. Secondly, official languages are very rarely used for ordinary (primary) purposes of communication in African societies, and when they are their use carries a specific social meaning. For instance, school children frequently employ English or French as a code language, when wanting to exclude uneducated children or adults. Although competence in the official language gives the speaker considerable social prestige, by virtue of its association with education, his emotional attachment belongs to his mother tongue; and wherever this cannot serve he prefers to use the local lingua franca in informal contacts. The use of the official language, even among those who are fully competent in it, is thus restricted by the rules of social behaviour to a few appropriate situations.[15]

For the individual citizen of a multilingual country the pattern of communication as described above seems to prescribe competence in at least three languages: his native language, the local lingua franca and the official language—the 'trifocal' pattern of language use observed by many sociolinguists. However, this prescription is modified by a number of other factors: by ethnic origin, by residence (rural versus urban), by the level of education, occupation and socio- economic aspirations. The majority of the traditional rural population, particularly those belonging to a numerically important ethnic group, are unlikely to need more than their native language. On the other hand, individuals from a minority group, who aspire to a high socio-economic position will need to learn one or two lingua francas in addition to the official language, while others whose native language happens to be the national lingua franca only have to acquire the official language. Seen in this perspective the options are not that different from those offered in many European countries, where dialects and socio-lects coexist side by side with the formal standard language, or where minorities have to be competent in the language of the majority. In both cases it is the acquisition of literacy itself: learning the complex formal styles of a written language and the 'elaborated code' of the educated spoken language, which consumes most time and effort.[16]

The functional specialisation of languages has both societal and linguistic consequences. From the point of view of linguistic development it implies that languages limited to one set of functions (e.g. at the level of in-group communication) will remain inadequate in their vocabulary and structure to express meanings related to the other sets of functions. At the same time, speakers of lingua francas and official languages are likely to have gaps of knowledge in these two types of languages when it comes to expressing meanings related to the sphere of the family and intimate relations, or the cultural content which is specific to their group of origin.

Each of these three types of languages also has its own social handicap. The official language—language of government and the élite, and hence associated with power and authority—is of little use when it is a question of appeals for solidarity. The official language inherited from the colonial times continues to imply the relations between rulers and ruled and is unlikely to encourage the development of democratic processes. Appeals to the electorate or government policy speeches couched in this language frequently invite the same type of resistance as did the authoritarian directives of the colonial administrators.

While multilingualism appears to be less troublesome for oral communication than is generally assumed, education and literacy in the same context introduce a whole new set of problems. As Goody & Watt (1972) have pointed out, the mere transition from an all-embracing oral culture to a literate culture has profound socio-cultural consequences.[17] The negative aspects of literacy can only be enhanced when it is a question of literacy in a foreign language, especially when this language is a symbol of domination. The argument commonly used in favour of education in the foreign official language evokes the principle of 'equal disadvantage', that is to say that in multilingual contexts none of the ethnolinguistic groups in a given country is advantaged over another with respect to government education. While this may be true to a certain extent, it merely shifts inequality to a different level: instead of inequality based on ethnic origin this system of education produces social inequality and inequality between the urban and rural population. However, as it promises to preserve the status quo for the present élite, whose class solidarity is evidently stronger than their ethnic solidarity, this system of education is by far the most popular in modern African countries.

The alternative, education in one or several local languages, is generally considered to be highly problematic. No country, least of all a poor developing country, can afford to multiply its educational expenses by providing teacher training, educational material and special classes for all its ethnolinguistic groups. The need to make choices in a social context which is always volatile is equally unattractive, and for these and other reasons progress in the various projects for 'mother tongue' education has been very slow.

In addition to the limited role which local languages are assigned in government education, most countries have adult literacy programmes, usually offered in a greater number of languages than those used in the school system, but these reach only a very small number of people and cannot be considered as a serious complement, let alone an alternative. This is particularly the case in countries where the indigenous languages are not used in the press, as this means that the newly acquired literacy has virtually no function and cannot be maintained. There is very little reliable information about the use of African languages in the media and more often than not, the reference to the use of a certain language in the press covers newsletters for religious congregations, occasional pamphlets on agricultural techniques or hygiene destined for the rural population and short but regular contributions to bilingual monthlies or weeklies, with the rare exception of a full-fledged daily newspaper.[18]

Last but not least, literacy cannot and must not have only utilitarian functions, such as the dissemination of knowledge via the written media; it also implies that the written language should be the natural mode of expression of an indigenous literature. So far, African writers have enriched the literature written in English and French with a number of great novels and poetry, while depriving their own peoples and languages of the gift of their imagination. Overcoming the effects of alienation and dedicating oneself to the development of an indigenous literature in Africa may prove to be a dangerous enterprise, as the experience of the Kenyan writer Ngugi Wa Thiong'o demonstrates. Having published a series of novels in English, for which he gained high esteem in his country, Ngugi turned to writing in his mother tongue (Gikuyu) and was imprisoned and eventually exiled as a result of this.[19]

There is another factor which enters into the debate about whether or not children should be educated in their mother tongue: it is the fear that literacy in previously unwritten local languages may have linguistic and behavioural consequences which may clash with the long-term goals of nation building. Wide-spread literacy tends to rigidify the orthography of a language and to slow down linguistic change, particularly at the grammatical level. Unwritten languages change more rapidly and, under favourable conditions and close contact, dialects and related languages may converge. One of the factors facilitating linguistic unification in Europe was the limited use of writing during the centuries of national consolidation before the invention of the printing press. In view of the inadequate advance of comparative linguistic studies in Africa today there is a danger that literacy may create separate languages, where in fact there is little more than dialect variation, and once a language is fixed in writing the kind of linguistic engineering which produced standard Shona in Zimbabwe will no longer be possible.[20]

Reading and writing change the relationship between the individual and his language: they externalise language and transform it into an object which can be contemplated. All this may endow the individual with a greater sense of separate identity and reinforce the barriers to forging a new supra-ethnic identity. Seen in this light literacy in the various smaller mother tongues might counteract any spontaneous convergence or prevent the adoption of a common national language. Even if such tendencies could be avoided with appropriate political education, there can be no doubt that linguistic fanaticism and separatism are more easily aroused in a literate society. Such consequences would be particularly deplorable in those countries where the tendency to adopt a single lingua franca is already well established.

Whenever language issues are discussed in multilingual African states, be it in order to select a certain number of indigenous languages for introduction in education, or to promote a lingua franca to the status of official language, such discussions invariably raise the spectre of tribalism and language conflict. For this reason it is imperative to analyse what lurks behind these fears and whether these types of conflict are really inherent and unavoidable in multilingual countries.

Notes to Chapter 5

1. UNESCO (1982, unpublished): Survey of Community Languages.
2. All sources consulted mention only that Kriol was generally acknowledged to be the principal medium of inter-ethnic communication, without giving any estimates.
3. The nine Nigerian languages given this status are: Fulani, Ibibo-Efik, Kanuri, Tiv, Ejo, Edo, Nupe, Igala and Idoma.
4. cf. Djite (1988b) and Lewis (1971).
5. cf. UNESCO (1982) and Gnielinski (1972).
6. cf. Sow (1977) and Boadi (1976).
7. e.g. among the countries having selected their *national languages*, Guinea includes two Tenda dialects spoken by 0.3% and 0.4% of the population total, whereas Niger's smallest national language is spoken by 7.3% of the population.
8. e.g. the UNESCO 'Meeting of experts on the use of the regional or subregional African languages as media of culture and communication within the continent', held in Bamako, 18–22 June 1979; and the UNESCO Survey of Community Languages (1982).
9. cf. Griffeth (1971).
10. cf. Heine (1970); Alexandre (1967) and Calvet (1981).
11. cf. Dalby (1969) and Tabouret-Keller (1971).
12. The following is a comparison between the percentage of Wolof speakers in Senegalese country towns and their surrounding rural district (Calvet & Wioland, 1967):
    Ziguinchor 80.04%—Ziguinchor district 17.33%
    Sedhiou 40.72%—Sedhiou district9.33%
    Kolda 27.81%—Kolda district 5%
    all three country towns are in Casamance, the province least affected by Wolof language spread.
13. The following are only two examples from the Wioland (1965) survey, reproducing the break-down tables of the pupils' ethnic background:
    DAKAR: 72.23% speak Wolof as first language = 47.82% both parents Wolof, 7%mother Wolof, 5.59% father Wolof, 11.82 neither parents Wolof.
    ZIGUINCHOR: 33.93% speak Wolof as first language = 8.83% both parents Wolof, 4.50% mother Wolof, 6.02% father Wolof, 14.58% neither parents Wolof
14. In a previous article, Mansour (1980), I suggested the term 'primary domain cluster' to embrace the domains family, friendship, market, street, work, village association, age-group, village councils, etc. for which African languages are used. I defined the 'secondary domain cluster' as the domains of administration, education, media or the modern economic sector (which require the use of foreign languages); secondary in the sense that socio-historically speaking it is a level of communication developed at a later stage, after the full development of the traditional functions of language in society. This distinction makes it clear

that African languages are perfectly adequate to express the traditional social functions of language, and that given time and opportunity, they will become equally adequate in this new set of functions.

15. cf. Parkin (1971), who observed a similar behaviour in the bars of Nairobi, where young men engaged in a joking competition in English, though otherwise they were using Swahili. cf. also Scotton (1982 a and b).

16. cf. the research into the causes of failure in the British school system done by Bernstein (1971). He came to the conclusion that a large section of the population (disadvantaged, poor, immigrant) were unable to handle the complex formal style of the written language ('elaborated code') which is the common medium of education.

17. As Goody & Watt (1972) have pointed out, the mere transition from the all-embracing oral culture to literacy has profound socio-cultural consequences involving alienation, a culture lag between lived experience and transmitted experience, as well as a gap between the illiterate and the literate sections of society.

18. According to the 1989 edition of *Africa South of the Sahara* there are two daily newspapers in Nigeria: *Amana* in Hausa and *Isokan* in Yoruba; the only other country in West Africa using a local language in a daily newspaper is Mauritania with *Ach-Chaab* appearing in Arabic and French. Even the list of weeklies is unimpressive. In Nigeria: *Albishir* and *Yancin Dan Adam* in Hausa, and *Eleti-Ofe* in Yoruba and English, *Irohin Yoruba*, *Irohin Imole* and *Gboung-boun* in Yoruba. In Ghana: Christian *Messenger* in English, Twi and Ga; in Mali: *Concorde* in Arabic and French; and in Liberia: *Lorma Weekly* in English and Lorma.

19. cf. Adams (1987).

20. The language now referred to as *Shona* (Zimbabwe) is the result of linguistic engineering (Doke, 1967) which started with a language survey in Southern Rhodesia in 1929. Linguists listed about 63 variations, grouped into six clusters, between five of which there was a high degree of mutual intelligibility. Doke and his team proceeded to the unification of these varieties. The five different orthographies of the missionaries were replaced by a commonly acceptable orthography, a standardised grammar based on the two most representative dialect clusters was produced, while for vocabulary purposes, words from two further clusters were drawn upon. The most important insight to be gained from this effort is that linguistic methods can be used towards achieving language unification, even though critics of this method say that Shona is a language which 'everyone writes and nobody speaks'—a comment which applies to virtually every written language!

6 The Role of Language in Internal Conflicts

Actual tribal societies have long since disappeared from most parts of Africa and what is generally referred to as 'tribalism' is the resistance of sub-national ethnolinguistic groups to incorporation into the larger national society. However, this term has also been used in connection with a particular group challenging the legitimacy of the national government, in which case we are dealing with a political phenomenon known wherever sub-national groups coexist, and where power is unequally distributed. Another aspect of 'tribalism' consists of a tendency to settle conflict between rival groups by force. The latter has become increasingly frequent, and not only between rival indigenous groups as in Spain, Yugoslavia or the Soviet Union, but between immigrant labour and their reluctant hosts in Britain and France. Only the term tribalism is never used in that context and is reserved for developing countries, to make us believe that we are dealing with a different phenomenon.

If African leaders are particularly conscious of the threat of tribalism this is partly due to the indoctrination received from the departing colonial administrators who upheld the old colonial myth that only their presence had prevented Africans from constantly being at each other's throat, and that they would never be able to govern themselves.

One of the numerous studies which link linguistic heterogeneity with national conflicts deserves mention here. Inglehart & Woodward (1972) consider that there is a relationship between political and economic development and the divisive effect of linguistic pluralism and that, in fact, this divisive effect will be greatest in a transitional phase 'when the masses are mobilised, but not yet assimilated'. Following this line of argument one should attempt to determine whether the masses in West African countries are still 'inert', in the sense of being illiterate and generally unaware of national events and without any expectations of social and economic mobility, or whether they are mobilised, but not yet assimilated into the national entity.

While the former category may, under the present circumstances, correspond more closely to the reality, this is obviously a small comfort to those concerned with language policy and language planning in African countries. The implication is that sooner or later there will be conflict—unless assimilation precedes mobilisation, hence it might be argued that changes in the status of official and education languages should be delayed as long as possible—a course of action which can only serve the interests of the present élite.

In order to get closer to a situation which may provoke ethnic conflict based on language issues (for that is what is meant by 'language conflict'), one should make an investigation of those countries where a change in the language policy has already taken place.

Language Policy and Ethnic Conflict in Mauritania

Mauritania is the only country in West Africa which undertook a major status change for one of its indigenous languages; in 1967 the Mauritanian government announced that Arabic would henceforth share the status of official language with French. How was this step received by the non-Arabic speaking ethnolinguistic minorities? Before we turn our attention to this question it is important to note that there is a problem concerning the demographic statistics. Official sources state that native speakers of Arabic make up 80% of the population, with the remaining 20% being split up into native speakers of Wolof (the largest group), and native speakers of Pulaar, Soninka and Bambara (Manding). However these figures are contested by the members of the minority groups.[1]

Mauritania and Senegal made headlines in 1989 because of a border incident which escalated into inter-ethnic violence in both countries between Mauritanians and Senegalese. Though that particular case was not an internal conflict, it was nourished from the same source: the troubled relationship between the Moors (descendants of Arabs and Berbers) and black Africans residing in Mauritania, compounded by French colonial policy. The Moors and West African tribes have been in contact for at least one thousand years, and in times of drought their competition over the fertile river flats of the Senegal river has become aggravated. The Moorish tribes were essentially nomads and lived on trade, considering themselves part of a greater Arabo-Berber unit with their roots deep in the Sahara and the Maghreb. The peasants and herdsmen of the Senegal valley and the southern oases were their major source of food and slave labour, a relationship which did not change much over the centuries (slavery was only recently officially abolished).

With the coming of colonial rule the fate of the non-Moorish population began to change. Mauritania was administered from St. Louis/Senegal (later from Dakar) and the colonial administration implemented the same policies on both sides of the river. When French schools were established the Moors boycotted them, considering western style education to be a dangerous attack on their traditional Islamic values. Meanwhile the black African population recognised in education a means of breaking out of their inferior status in relation to the Moors. As independence approached, and because the river itself was recognised as the border between the two countries, a sizeable population of ethnically Senegalese became Mauritanian citizens, and many Moors remained in Senegal where they had a monopoly on the small retail trade of basic food items. In Mauritania members of the minority groups took up a disproportionate number of important positions and gained influence, since it was mainly these who had availed themselves of western education, held the diplomas and had the skills needed for the administration of a modern state, while the Moorish aristocracy reserved the main political positions for themselves. In 1967 these Arabic speaking politicians raised Arabic to equal status with French as the second official language. The next step, arabisation of education, caused considerable unrest among the minority groups. Their privileged position was wedded to the privileged position of French—hence they demanded maintenance of French as the language of education and, at a later stage, also demanded equal consideration for their own languages.

Here then, it seems that the protesting minority groups were indeed mobilised, particularly through a proportionately greater exposure to education, and not assimilated into the majority group. The conflict also appears to have been caused by language policy, since the project of switching to Arabic as the main language of education provoked demonstrations in 1978/79. At the same time it seemed clear to the unbiased observer that the change in language and education policy was either a pretext for giving vent to other social grievances, or that the reaction was manipulated by francophile interest groups and possibly it was a mixture of both. Most members of the minority groups had been living in close contact with the Moors and had at least a superficial command of the spoken language (i.e. the Hassaniya dialect of Arabic). Considering that the acquisition of Modern Standard Arabic is not unlike learning a second language for the illiterate native speaker, the disadvantages of the non-native speakers appear to be so slight that it should be cancelled by the advantage of using a language which is at least familiar and culturally integrated.

It is more likely that this hostile reaction had other, essentially social and economic causes. Throughout the 1980s the tension has been growing due to the distribution of newly irrigated land which became available after the completion of the Manantali dam. Most of this went to big agro-business run by the Moors, while the traditional peasants of the Senegal valley (Wolof, Tukulor and others) went empty-handed. It is therefore not surprising that the economically disadvantaged groups suspect any other government policy of further eroding their position. After a failed coup-d'état in 1987 mounted by the *Front de libération des Africains de Mauritanie* followed by a purge of black civil servants and officers, and the mounting anxiety among the Moors concerning the much higher birthrate among the minority groups, the recent outbreak of violence does not come as a surprise. There can be little doubt that the language policy aggravated the situation in Mauritania, but it was certainly not its cause. This became particularly clear after the events of 1989, which were in no way related to language policy, but most certainly were an expression of economic and social frustration and pent-up anger against those sections of the population which were perceived as being advantaged.

Language Issues and the Nigerian Civil War

Nigeria, the most populous and economically most powerful country in West Africa was torn by a civil war which lasted three years and almost led to the secession of 'Biafra' (the name the secessionists wanted to give to the independent Eastern Region). This event shook the whole of Africa because of its violence and the dangerous chain reactions it might have triggered off. The immediate events leading up to this attempt at secession and civil war were two successive coups d'état in 1966: the first one abolishing the loose federation of four Nigerian states and establishing a centralised military government under an Ibo general whose main advisers were Ibo officers; the second headed by another general (Gowon) whose main remedy for Nigeria's ills was a proposal to reconstitute Nigeria as a federation of 12 states under a presidential system.

However, the emotions which fuelled the war had their roots in decades of unequal development, prejudice, nepotism and hostilities, particularly in the relation between the Northerners (Hausa–Fulani) and Ibos from the Eastern Region, which ended in the massacre of Ibo civil servants and workers in the Northern Region in 1966. Ibo reaction was a withdrawal into the Eastern Region, rejection of the 12-states-plan which stipulated the division of the Eastern Region into three states, thereby removing minority territories and the major oil fields from Ibo control, and declaration of secession.

A vivid description of the socio-cultural background to the crisis is given by Lloyd (1970). One fact ought to be kept in mind when analysing the Nigerian crisis: the Hausa, Yoruba and Ibo populations each outnumber the populations of most independent African countries (the estimates he cites for that period are: Hausa 15 million native speakers, Yoruba 10 million and Ibo 10 million). The Hausa language belongs to the Chadic language group; Yoruba and Ibo belong to the same language family (Kwa), but the linguistic distance between them was compared to that between English and Russian. Furthermore, linguistic distance between these three groups is paralleled by an equally considerably difference in socio-cultural development. The pre-colonial Hausa–Fulani emirates had a complex social hierarchy similar to that in medieval Europe, with their walled cities being centres of trade and administration for the surrounding rural district. The Hausa are Muslim and strictly traditional in their life style and general philosophy, with an apathetic peasantry ruled by an arrogant aristocracy. Pre-colonial Ibo society was in every sense the opposite to Hausa society: an egalitarian village society which did not recognise any form of central authority. The Ibos were animist and fiercely independent in spirit, even in relation to their own elders. Yoruba kingdoms were somewhere in between these two extremes, with their towns and more complex social organisation. The northern Yoruba who had come into contact with the Hausa, had become Muslim; while the Southerners were animist, like the Ibos, and eventually converted to Christianity.

The most outstanding feature of Nigeria's colonial history was Britain's experiment with 'indirect rule' started in the Hausa–Fulani emirates of northern Nigeria, and later carried over to the Yoruba territories and, less successfully, to the Ibo territories. Between 1922 and 1963 the separate provincial governments for the northern, western and eastern regions consolidated and deepened the already existing fundamental cultural and social differences between the three main ethnolinguistic groups, and helped to create some degree of internal cohesion within each region.

In the early phase of colonial rule the British administration concerned itself purely with the economic aspects and the maintenance of law and order, while education was left to the missionaries. These were very active in the south, using mainly the Yoruba and Ibo language in their mission work but were not permitted to operate in the Muslim north. When in 1922 a system of secular education was established, it was based on the missionaries' experience in education through the mother tongues with gradual transition to English, but each Region had its own ministry for education and tended to reinforce the values of its dominant ethnic group. Thus education in the Northern Region took care not to come into conflict with Islamic tradition and the social caste system, and went little beyond some basic teaching of English and arithmetic, while the Western and Eastern Regions followed the pattern of British education more closely.

As a result the three ethnic groups developed different attitudes towards modernisation: the Ibos were the most motivated and most open to western ideas, technical innovation and the construction of a new society, with the Yoruba taking a similar stance. While the northern emirs tried to retard independence, it was the educated Ibo élite which led the struggle for independence and became the centre of Nigerian nationalism and Pan-Africanism.[2] In the end the Northerners were persuaded by economic exigencies (such as the problem of transport for their land-locked region) to join the federation, but only with the intention of dominating it. The shift to plural democracy only aggravated the problem, as political parties tended to be formed along ethnic lines, and in the absence of any distinct political ideology, used simplistic ethnic arguments in their election campaigns.[3]

An additional factor contributing to ethnic strife was the competition for power and wealth in the form of positions in the civil service. The modernisation and nigerianisation of the administration in the 1950s had brought the better educated Southerners, often of humble peasant origin, into conflict with the traditional Hausa–Fulani aristocracy who lacked qualifications, but considered these positions to be their prerogatives. As the rapid expansion of educational and employment opportunities of the 1950s was followed by sudden stagnation and a surplus of educated personnel in the mid-1960s, it brought Ibo and Yoruba into intense rivalry in the federal services and universities, leading to accusations of nepotism—more often justified than not—and hostilities. Hence the first coup in 1966, originally an anti-corruption coup supported by both Ibo and Yoruba, was eventually interpreted as an Ibo take-over move.

In the centre of the Nigerian conflict with its triangle of hostilities: Northerners versus Southerners (in particular Ibo) and Ibo versus Yoruba, language issues did not play an important role. While colonial education policy in each region had resulted in the use of Hausa Yoruba and Ibo in education up to middle school, educational policy in the period immediately after independence favoured early education in English. Hence the greater mobility of the educated southern élite did not at first lead to conflicting interests in education.

On the other hand, one of the side issues of the Nigerian conflict was the position of the minority groups in each region. At first this led to the creation of a fourth state in 1963 and, when a new impetus was given to mother tongue education the minority groups in the regions concerned voiced their opposition to the dominance of Hausa, Yoruba and Ibo. In this case language issues were pushed into the foreground although, as usual, they were only one of the causes for discontent. Indeed, the creation of twelve states in 1968 was in part an answer to the minority problem, and new state boundaries were drawn to correspond more closely to ethno-linguistic boundaries.

What are the conclusions to be drawn from the Nigerian conflict concerning the role of language in internal conflicts? Firstly, it would appear futile to attempt to separate language attitudes from social attitudes, since in any situation where a strong sense of ethnic identity has developed, language is the symbol of this identity. Secondly, wherever people become conscious of a serious social conflict, but for a number of reasons are unable to voice their problems directly, language may become an issue. Especially in developing countries which are host to a league of social problems: poverty, unequal development, corruption, nepotism, and where social unrest, if not actually manifest , is always just below the boiling point, an unpopular language policy favouring the use of a particular language over others could easily upset the delicate balance and trigger off a conflict.

Thirdly, the present situation of latent social unrest in most developing countries is the logical consequence of past neglect, or more often of a deliberate colonial policy. In Nigeria, for instance, British administration had fostered the separate development of the three regions and must have been well aware of the forces pulling in different directions. If there had been more concern for the future stability of Nigeria, the emerging leadership might have been better advised to opt for greater autonomy within a confederate system. The position of the minority groups in each of the virtually autonomous states would not have been any different from elsewhere in Africa, in that the pressure exercised by the dominant groups might have favoured eventual assimilation. The research carried out by Osaji (1979) seems to suggest that the process of language spread of Hausa in the Northern Region, both as lingua franca and through assimilation and language shift, was sufficiently advanced to guarantee its continuation.[4] Under these circumstances the goal of national unity would have had a greater chance of being realised within the former Northern Region, and possibly within the Western and Eastern Regions likewise, than it had under the centralised military government of 1966. However, with the creation of twelve states in 1968 Nigeria set out on a different path, the path to a more pluralist society which gives attention to the various demands of its many ethnic groups. The details of this policy will be discussed in Chapter 8.

To conclude this examination of the role of language in internal conflicts—there seem to be three main causes which are only indirectly linked to language issues:

(a) the spread of western style education which becomes the key to social promotion in the modern context; (While the ambitious cannot afford to reject this type of education in itself, any policy which threatens to give advantages to one group over another, such as the choice of one rather than another African language as medium of education, arouses fear, brings about defensive behaviour, and reaffirms ethno-centric sentiments and language loyalty. How such fears can be allayed will be the subject of the following chapter.)

(b) the fact that internal conflict is considerably exacerbated by the practice of corruption and nepotism, prevalent among the present authoritarian regimes in Africa;

(c) the socio-economic problems in developing countries which sharpen the competition between individuals as well as between groups and tend to awaken the collective memory of past injustices and exploitation suffered at the hand of a rival ethnic group.

This type of social behaviour is by no means limited to developing countries in general, nor to Africa in particular. After many centuries of deliberate assimilation policies and attempts at national integration in European countries, minority ethnic groups are once again demanding their language rights. It seems as though it had been precisely these attempts at enforced assimilation which strengthened the minorities' resistance and led to the maintenance of languages long believed to be extinct.

What then are the options for multilingual African countries? Should their authorities plan for assimilation and linguistic unification or for the establishment of a democratic pluralist system within which the rights of minorities could be guaranteed? And if so, are there blueprints for a successful, non-conflictual transition? And how long can a 'go-safe–no-change' language policy be maintained? These are questions on which the following chapters focus.

Notes to Chapter 6

1. The UNESCO Survey of Community Languages (1982) mentions 60% Arabic speakers and 40% native speakers of the various African languages. cf. also Bessis (1989) who reports that an estimated 50% of the Mauritanian population are of black African descent.
2. cf. also Peshkin (1967).
3. cf. Lloyd (1970) ...'Thus, at the grass roots level, AG politicians often assert that an NCNC victory in Western Nigeria would mean that the Yoruba would be

ruled by the Ibo..'. In addition the minorities in each region were used for political manipulation: when the Yoruba-based AG campaigned in the north to gain support from the northern minorities, the Hausa-based NPC used religious-cultural arguments in defence and presented the AG as a threat to Islamic values and accused them of wanting to undermine society with alcoholism and debauchery.

4. The author presents the situation of Hausa in the former Northern Region as follows: in the 1970s Hausa was spoken by almost 100% of the population (the Fulani being bilingual) in four states—Kano, Kaduna, Sokoto and Bauchi. In the states Kwara, Niger, Plateau and Benue some populations had undergone complete language shift to Hausa, in other parts 50%, 25% or 10% spoke Hausa as lingua franca. In the state Gongola Hausa speakers made up between 10–25% of the population. The only strong resistance to the spread of Hausa was registered in Borgu, which had only about 1% Hausa speakers, the majority language being Kanuri. Yoruba and Ibo speakers likewise resisted the spread of Hausa. Osaji estimated the total of Hausa speakers to be 25 million, or about 32% of the national total.

7 Policy Options: Assimilationist or Pluralist?

Before approaching the question of policy options it is necessary to diverge for a moment in order to re-examine the social functions of language in the context of supra-ethnic social organisations of which the modern nation is a form. While the relationship between tribe and language was a simple one-to-one relationship where one defined the other, language acquired new functions in more complex social organisations. New collectivities were created—frequently by force—which had none of the characteristics of tribal society and were made up of diverse components.

The most frequent reaction to this situation in modern history has been an attempt to enforce assimilation and 'forge' unity through policies which suppress linguistic and other differences. The present wave of demands by linguistic minorities in European nations, long considered to be monolingual and socially integrated, led the search for a case of successful language imposition far afield: to the spread of the Arabic language which followed in the wake of the Arab conquest in the 7th and 8th century. The unique conditions which favoured assimilation and language shift in that case help to focus on possible reasons for failure elsewhere.

There are very few cases where a pluralist solution was attempted before the second half of the 19th century, and Switzerland is an example which yields many important insights. The Swiss example inspired the Soviet language policy of the 1920s, and the ups and downs of the latter likewise provide a useful lesson for policy makers and language planners in multilingual countries.

Language as Symbol of Social Identity and Means of Social Control

Parallel to its basic and universal function of communication language serves at the same time to delimit the possibilities of contact, originally to the clan or tribal group. Hence, in simple societies where there is not much that distinguishes one community from another it forms the most powerful

100

symbol of social identity. In situations where two or more communities compete for scarce resources the maintenance of linguistic differences is part of the survival mechanism of the group. This is particularly striking when the linguistic differences are minor dialect variations and where the possibility of large-scale communication is maintained.

In the case of high-level linguistic differences communication with neighbouring groups is more easily controlled and usually restricted to a few bilingual intermediaries. However, if close cooperation between neighbouring ethno-linguistic groups is in the interest of all concerned, large sections of their communities may become bilingual. In such situations of equality—not necessarily equality of size but a similar level of socio-economic development so that each community is equally able to protect its members—there are no positive or negative values attached to languages. Mother tongues are the symbol of social identity and other languages are viewed neutrally and pragmatically, that is to say as a means of social communication. There is no ambivalence since social identity is not questioned and need not be defended. Even rivalry and hostility between neighbouring groups does not affect this 'symmetric' perception of languages.[1]

In many parts of West Africa where symmetric sociolinguistic relations were predominant this situation changed drastically with the advent of colonialism, which replaced symmetric relations by a complex hierarchy of languages. Even before that, during the period of European coastal trade, the development of Pidgins and Creoles, as well as the use of interpreters taken from major African trader clans, transformed those languages into valuable social assets. The knowledge of such languages, above all the knowledge of the colonial language, thus became a means of exerting power. The African interpreter assisting a colonial official not only exercised control over who got access to him, but also over what facts would reach him through his interpretation. In this way language acquired a further function: that of providing access to power, social prestige and the financial rewards that are associated with it.

The contradictions between the identity function of language, its ability to express and evoke solidarity, and its power function are at the root of all ambivalent attitudes towards coexisting languages which have filled so many pages of sociolinguistic literature. For example, to understand the language behaviour and attitudes of the Tunisian élite, as described by Stevens (1983) one only needs to ask the question: which of the three coexisting linguistic varieties fulfils the power function in the post-colonial context? Certainly not the Tunisian dialect of Arabic, nor Classical Arabic—even though this is considered to be a prestige language. French alone is associated with modernity, authority and power. And through language policy (Stevens mentions that though education is bilingual, French takes up 70% of the curriculum by the end of secondary school and more at university) entry into the ranks of the élite is tightly controlled. Why does the Tunisian élite (and other Third World élites) consider their own mother tongue to be inferior? Because it does not provide them with access to power, and since the main goal of an élite is to remain in power and to give their children the same chances, such an attitude is not very surprising. Furthermore, they have been brain-washed by western education into believing that this inferiority is inherent and cannot be mended.

The split between the identity/solidarity function and the power function of language is not purely an African or Third World phenomenon. It is equally well demonstrated in situations where the written standard language is juxtaposed to a socially inferior dialect.[2] Although generally there are strong pressures to conform to the norms of the standard language (through education and the media) and, despite the fact that the acceptance of such norms would constitute the first step on the ladder to social promotion, many people continue to cling to their low-status dialects. In fact, contrary to all expectations, the use of 'Black English' seems to be increasing since American sociolinguists first took an interest in this phenomenon in the late 1960s. Studies on the maintenance of low- status dialects show that this phenomenon correlates with lack of social mobility, and reinforces the network system of mutual support. Thus the identity function of language gains increased importance as part of a survival strategy in the face of exploitation and marginalisation.

There are other reasons why exploited minority groups react negatively to attempts at assimilation. Many a language policy which is assimilationist on the surface in fact serves to exclude sections of the community, to place them in a situation of permanent exploitation. For instance, the US has a long history of discriminatory legislation where, under the pretext of assimilation, language is used as a means of controlling and limiting the number of those to be assimilated. Between the mid-nineteenth century and 1965 literacy in English was the precondition for being granted suffrage, a law which effectively barred first- and often second-generation migrants, Blacks and Native Americans. With regard to naturalisation a similar practice was selectively applied until, in 1950, it became written law (Internal Security Act). Another method used for discriminatory purposes was the practice of setting entry exams for government service and private business, including for manual labour, which was legal until 1920 and used illegally for a long time after that.[3]

This leads us to the phenomenon of persisting loyalties to minority languages in the old nations of Europe, a phenomenon which may have serious implications for multinational countries, particularly in the Third World. The function of social control enters into the very concept of a 'minority'. The members of small but autonomous linguistic communities would not think of themselves as minorities *vis-à-vis* their bigger neighbours. A minority is defined as such by the group which wields the power over it, which has incorporated it in its state structure. In Europe there is hardly a country which does not contain within its borders minority populations, which for centuries have quietly resisted assimilation until the second half of this century, when minority language rights became a political issue.

The question which many people ask is: why does this happen now, when thanks to universal education (in the majority languages) virtually every adult is bilingual and many of the younger generation no longer speak the minority language of their ancestors? In part this apparent return to provincialism and particularism may be a sign that assimilationist language policies did not in fact produce the social mobility that they seemed to promise, that the hurdles were too high and the number of those failing to take them too great. Particularly in a general climate of democracy and respect for human rights the automatic imposition of the majority language as the sole language of education and local government is perceived as an aggression against the minority groups' sense of socio-cultural identity.

But again, identity is only the surface issue, only one side of the coin, the other being the question of language controlling access to power. A Basque, for instance, who is excluded from positions of authority and power in his own village or town, on the basis of exams held in Spanish or French, while these positions go to native speakers of those languages, feels disinherited, like a servant in his own house. And, as we know from history, the disinherited eventually engage in a struggle—class struggle, national struggle or liberation struggle—in order to regain what they consider to be rightfully theirs.

On the other hand, there is evidence that the importance of language as an identity marker dwindles in the presence of real opportunities for social mobility and tangible rewards linked to language shift. Here we need only mention the decline of regional dialects and the diminishing interest in a number of dying languages. The case of Irish is particularly interesting in this context. After centuries of English rule and imposition of the English language Irish became the rallying cry of Irish nationalists and, since 1893, but particularly since independence in 1922, great efforts were made to revive, modernise and reintroduce the Irish language; yet it seems that this policy has been a failure.[4] Only about 4% of the population of Ireland use Irish extensively , though 25% report that they know it well. While legislation is published in Irish and English, almost all official business is conducted in English. This contrasts with a revival of Irish among the Catholic population of Ulster, where it had previously disappeared, but where its symbolic function in the struggle against British dominance is once again needed.

On the basis of the preceding discussion of the twin functions of language it becomes clear that linguistic identification with a sub-national collectivity is essentially the result of socio-economic and political pressures. When society is split into two diametrically opposed classes: the rulers and the ruled, maintenance of linguistic differences are merely a signal that social cleavages exist. The more emphasis is placed on the power function of language, in the sense that the acquisition of a prestige variety is the prerequisite for economic success and political participation—the greater the gap between the two classes and the two linguistic varieties. Sociolinguists usually refer to such a rigid hierarchy of languages as 'diglossia'.[5]

A society where language has only its original identity function and where several languages or varieties may coexist symmetrically, without forming part of a hierarchy is either pre-modern, pre-capitalist or consequentially pluralist and egalitarian in its inter- ethnic relations.

The Relationship between Language and Nation

Many writers have grappled with the term *nation* and sought to define it in the modern context, yet in common usage it has remained fluid and ambiguous. Sometimes it is used as a synonym for 'country', an entity which has a precise geographic location and an independent state structure, as in the compound 'United Nations'. At other times it seems to refer to entities which have no politico-economic realisation, but only a cultural–linguistic one, such as the Arab nation which refers to the totality of countries in which Arabic is the native language and whose people have a common history and common cultural values.

In view of the fact that the majority of the members of the United Nations are multi-ethnic and multilingual, a discussion of the relationship between language and nation would have to come to terms with the politico-economic aspect of that term rather than its purely cultural, linguistic interpretation.

The old nations of Europe (England, France, Spain) were states long before they became nations in the linguistic sense. Languages were not the criteria in their formation and linguistic unification rarely became an issue in these monarchies which derived the legitimacy of their rule from divine right. Language imposition on their dominions was at first almost automatic until it became conscious policy in the struggle against separatist tendencies at the dawn of capitalism. In France a conscious assimilationist policy was again enforced following the French revolution in order to prevent the country from falling apart. Yet linguistic unification in those nations has only been achieved on the surface, and minority languages as well as regional dialects persist.

Most other nations of Europe are what Fishman (1972) calls 'nation-states', in contrast to the former 'state-nations', namely those who gained statehood in the 19th and early 20th century, basing their claim on a common nationality as defined by language. Undoubtedly, these various forms of linguistic nationalism were influenced by 19th century German philosophers, but it is equally important to remember the aspect of their struggle for liberation. As part of the Austro-Hungarian, Russian or Ottoman Empires their languages and cultures had been suppressed while the languages of the rulers had assumed the power function. The desire to return to earlier structures where the two functions of language were combined in one and the same language does not require great leaps into philosophy, nor does the determination to cast off alien bonds.

The literal interpretation of the *principle of nationalities*, the principle that 'each language group, however small, somehow has the right, duty and destiny to become a sovereign state'[6] inevitably created new problems. Such claims gave rise to a debate about what constitutes a nationality, or rather, who has the right to independent nationhood and who does not. Those who based their claim on a common historical past, having at some stage lost their political independence, were generally considered to have a legitimate cause, while others were branded 'ahistoric' and hence had their claims ridiculed and initially suppressed. Yet, linguistic nationalism with or without the component of historical legitimacy was obviously not sufficient cause. The main reasons why such countries as Greece, Hungary, Poland and Finland were able to gain independent statehood was not related to any quality inherent in their culture and language; nor was it because of their 'will to nationhood' and 'realisation of common destiny', but because the multi-ethnic empires of which they had formed a part were disintegrating. As the various claims to nationhood threatened the status quo it was in the interest of the ruling class to arrive at a definition which would enable them to label the distinct groups in their countries as *national minorities*, and thus re-channel the dispute into the issue of granting civil equality and rights concerning the use of the minority language. This way a challenge to the power of the state was avoided.

The other side of the debate on nationality was led by Marx, Engels and their followers who rejected the mysticism of language-based nationalism and recognised nationalist struggles as essentially struggles for seizing power over the state apparatus, and hence a type of class struggle. Marx also introduced the concept of viability, namely that a collectivity claiming independent statehood should be viable economically and have a sizeable population. By implication, therefore, Marx and Engels were opposed to the 'principle of nationalities' as an absolute rule.

A much more clear-cut definition was proposed by Stalin in 1913:

A nation is a human group which possesses certain definite charac-teristics. It is a historically stable community of people. It has a com-mon vernacular language. It occupies a single piece of territory. It has an integrated, coherent economy. It possesses a community of psycho-logical make-up (a folk-psychology, or national character). And it is a historical category belonging to a definite epoch, the epoch of rising capitalism.[7]

These words were written before the Bolshevik revolution and their main aim was to maintain unity in the struggle for socialism. While certain large nationalities in the Russian Empire were considered to have legitim-ate claims to autonomy, others, particularly the scattered groups (among them the Jews) had no such claim since they had no 'single piece of territory' and no 'integrated economy'. In other words, Stalin's definition also served to distinguish *nationalities* from *national minorities*, a practice closely followed by later Soviet language policy which will be discussed in Chapter 7.

Few of the countries obtaining independent statehood since 1945 corre-spond to Stalin's definition of nationality. Language ceased to be a defining criterion and the majority of Third World countries which became inde-pendent in this period are multilingual. In fact, none of the criteria as outlined by Stalin have continued to play a role, except for the 'single piece of territory', as defined by the departing colonial powers.

Just as the word 'nation' underwent a semantic shift, its derivative 'nationalist' as referring to the élites of colonies struggling for inde-pendence gained a different meaning. The new nationalist leaders were only rarely able to use a vernacular language to mobilise the masses and their rhetoric was primarily anti-colonialist, anti-imperialist and only sec-ondarily concerned with reasserting authentic values. Yet the 19th century model of 'one nation one language' continues to haunt policy makers in newly independent countries, along with great chunks of undigested and totally inappropriate western ideology. The analysis of a historical case of unification through language (and religion) may therefore help to focus on what kind of processes this involves.

Successful Assimilation: The Case of Arabic

History abounds in examples of conquerors attempting to impose their languages upon the conquered people, but many of these were short- lived and few succeeded in creating a new homogeneous society through the processes of assimilation and language shift. The spread of Arabic in the wake of the Muslim conquest is one of the success stories which demonstrates what social factors are favourable to widespread and lasting language shift.

Modern Standard Arabic developed from the dialect of an Arabian tribe (the Quraysh) ruling the city of Mecca and its environs. By the beginning of the Islamic era (622 AD) it had already developed into a lingua franca, intelligible to most of the nomadic tribes of the Arab peninsula. During the early phase of the victories of the Arab–Muslim armies in Syria, Palestine, Egypt, Iraq and Persia, the Arab conquerors were greatly outnumbered and their language inadequate for the administration of such vast territories and peoples speaking many languages. Thus they were obliged to use the languages of the two empires from which they had conquered these territories for this purpose, i.e. Greek in Egypt, Palestine and Syria and Persian in Iraq and the eastern provinces. Had it not been for the Qur'an and the tradition that Islam and the Arabic language were inseparable, the Arab conquerors would most likely have been absorbed and their language given way to the major languages of the conquered peoples. As it was, the driving forces behind the conquest were initially the liberation of Arabs who had previously migrated to these parts and who were subjected, and the propagation of Islam which went hand in hand with a process of social transformation and arabisation.

Indeed, the khalifs of this great multilingual empire considered it to be one of their tasks to preserve the Arabic language and to protect it against corrupting influences. With the conversion of large sections of the population to Islam there came a great demand for instruction in Arabic and as a result of this the first grammar books and teaching manuals were compiled in the reign of the 4th khalif Ali, only 25 years after the beginning of the conquest. Under the khalif Abd-al-Malik (685–705) it became official policy to write all public registers in Arabic (instead of Greek or Persian) and Arabic thus became the official language. As a result of this many more people studied Arabic in order to be eligible for public office.

Under the Umayyads the Arabs conquered the rest of North Africa and Spain, and the eastern provinces now included Transcaucasia and Transoxiana (i.e. the south of the present Soviet Union)) and stretched as far as present Pakistan. In Spain Arabic was instituted as the official language from the beginning of Muslim rule (710 AD). The 8th century saw a steady expansion of Arabic throughout the conquered territories through conversion and assimilation of the local populations and, at least at the level of public and intellectual life, Arabic had become the dominant language from the Atlantic to the Indus in little over a century.

The 9th and 10th centuries were the golden age of Arabic civilisation, with an extraordinary blossoming of literature, science and all fields of scholarship. The knowledge of Greece and the ancient orient was absorbed and their works translated into Arabic. By this time, the majority of intellectuals writing in Arabic in the many centres of learning were of non-Arab origin, though generally they gave themselves Arab names. This and the sheer volume of intellectual output testifies to the extent of successful arabisation.

However, the weak points in the Empire soon emerged with the beginning of the 11th century. The reconquest of Spain started to push back the Arabic language until at the end of the 15th century it had disappeared from western Europe. The eastern provinces, which had never been entirely arabised, were conquered by the Turkish speaking Seljuqs who restored Persian as the official language. And though many intellectuals continued to write in Arabic, only the Arabic script and a large component of Arabic loan words remained in the Turkish, Persian, Afghan and north Indian languages—and this essentially through the influence of Islam which remained the main religion in that area.

As a phenomenon of language shift Arabic owes a great deal of its success to its link with a nascent universal religion which, moreover, was in its most dynamic phase at a point in history when the old empires were in a state of decadence and decline. The new faith was able to capture the wave of widespread social upheaval and give it a direction and purpose. The Islamic state offered security and a moral order based on the principles of freedom, equality and tolerance of the various forms of Christianity as well as Judaism. Contrary to the prevalent western image the advancing Arabs did not convert 'by the sword'. It was the laws of the Muslim state which provided incentives to conversion and assimilation by offering tax advantages and access to social promotion. In addition to this the Arabs formed not only the ruling class; their soldiers, recruited from the ever-hungry nomadic clans of the Arabian peninsula, frequently received land in lieu of payment. These either settled and mingled with the local peasants or leased their land and joined the mixed urban population, which in turn helped to speed up the process of language shift to Arabic.[8]

Among the important lessons to be learned from this example is the lesson that assimilation and language shift may, under the right historical, social and cultural conditions, become the most attractive and most rewarding choice for the conquered populations. However, this favourable confluence of circumstances is relatively rarely found on such a large scale. Furthermore, the process of assimilation undoubtedly works best when it is entirely voluntary and not handicapped by either prejudice or attempts at exploitation on the part of the ruling sociolinguistic group.

The Swiss Model of Linguistic Pluralism

Switzerland, the country which has virtually invented some of the mechanism of modern federalism, is Europe's oldest and most stable multilingual country. The original three Swiss–German cantons which broke away from Habsburg domination in 1291 established a confederation which was soon joined by neighbouring likewise German-speaking cantons. By the end of the 15th century there were 13 cantons, including the group of Raeto-Romansh speakers which form now the smallest linguistic group. The independence of the confederation of 13 cantons was recognised at the end of the 15th century and it was subsequently joined by neighbouring French cantons and the Italian Ticino which considered this move a more acceptable alternative to annexation attempts by France and Italy.

It was due to the fact of this voluntary association that, from the beginning, the linguistic communities and languages of Switzerland had equal rights. Thus Switzerland escaped from one of the major problems of newly formed federations: how to establish equality between populations of different sizes and different previous social statuses, and between languages at different stages of development.

An important principle in Swiss federalism is the territorial principle, that is to say that in most cases the territory of the cantons coincides with linguistic boundaries, thus creating monolingual units. Each canton has legislative and administrative autonomy and its language is used in all domains of social communication. As a result the German speaking cantons do not represent a power block and are in fact linguistically subdivided into distinct dialect groups.

Bilingual cantons have administrative sub-units to give each linguistic community as much autonomy and sense of security as possible. As recently as 1979 a new French canton (Jura) was carved out of the bilingual canton Bern in response to popular demand. Where separate administrative units are not feasible, for instance in bilingual towns such as Fribourg and Bienne, separate educational facilities are available for each linguistic group—or at least separate classes—following a different curriculum and being separately administered. Only senior technical colleges and universities combine students of all linguistic groups, where the language of instruction is determined by each individual lecturer. Students are expected to be bilingual, after the compulsory study of a second language (French or German) at school.

However, among the population in general there is little effort to promote active bilingualism or closer cultural contact. Active bilingualism is restricted to the agencies of the federal government in Bern and big business such as banks and insurance companies whose employees are required to be fluent in French and German. In fact these two languages were chosen to be the official languages for the federal government and for communications between the cantons and the federal government. The Italian canton opted to use French and the Romansh speakers use German for this purpose.

The territorial principle, though leading to separatism, or perhaps because of it, has had the effect of eliminating tension and stabilising linguistic zones despite widespread migration; because migrating individuals accept the fact that, by moving to a different monolingual canton, they give up their linguistic rights and generally are quickly assimilated. This has proved particularly important in view of the numerical strength and proclivity for migration of the German speaking majority. The only exception to the territorial principle applies to French civil servants of the federal government in German speaking Bern, for whose children a French school is available.

In addition the constitution provides that each individual, no matter in which canton he resides, has the right to address federal government agencies in his mother tongue and will receive an answer in that language.

The combination of all these factors—juridical equality, the territorial principle operating within the framework of a loose federal system and the principle of individual language rights—seem to have defused possible conflict by creating a socio-psychological safety net. The existence and continuation of each linguistic group as a social unit, and hence the individual's social identity, are not perceived to be threatened. On the other hand, pluralism in Switzerland relies on separate coexistence. There are no overt or covert plans for future closer integration or assimilation, nor is Swiss pluralism aimed at reducing the stereotyped prejudices prevalent between the other nations of Europe. In fact they seem to be more pronounced.[9]

Last, but not least, the absence of ethnic conflict in Switzerland is equally due to its economic stability and prosperity: when the cake is big enough every partner can be relatively content with his share. This important factor is absent in the multilingual countries of eastern Europe and the Third World. While the Swiss model of pluralism may serve as an inspiration for other multilingual countries, it would be unwise to underestimate the positive role of the economic factor and the effect of 500 years of common history.

Pluralist Language Policy in the Soviet Union[10]

In the first decade of this century the sociolinguistic situation in the collapsing Russian empire had certain aspects in common with African countries on the threshold of independence. Tsarist Russia was a multi-ethnic and multilingual colonial empire with Russian as its official language, despite the fact that of the approximately 130 languages, 20 had their own writing system and literary tradition. How Soviet language planners dealt with this situation is therefore of vital interest for other multilingual countries.

The ideological basis of Soviet language policy is Lenin's statement in the Communist Party Program of 1919, that all nationalities irrespective of size have equal rights, that all languages irrespective of the stage of linguistic development are equal, that the right to have children educated in their native tongue is a basic right, and that Russian has no claim to be granted a special status. In his stand on language policy Lenin was strongly influenced by Switzerland. Both Lenin and Stalin (during his earlier period as the head of the Soviet state) were firmly committed to the linguistic development and cultural revalorisation of all the written and unwritten national languages and Lenin, personally, was strongly opposed to using the Cyrillic script for non-Russian languages, calling it 'the alphabet of autocratic oppression, of missionary propaganda of Great Russian chauvinism'.

The other dominant principle which many western scholars tend to misunderstand and consider contradictory with the first, is the conviction, basic to Marxism, that nationalism and nationalist manifestations are harmful to the goal of constructing a new socialist society in which all differences should eventually be abolished. However, Lenin stated explicitly that *forced assimilation must at all cost be avoided* and that economic and social relationships would, of their own, create the need and desire to use a common language, one which is most suitable for the majority.[11] Hence, the Leninist/Stalinist formula for Soviet language policy — 'national in form and socialist in content' — has to be seen as the expression of a long-term goal, namely the ultimate fusion of the Soviet nationalities.

Meanwhile the principle of nationalities was guiding the immediate policy needs.

In this context it is of vital importance for an understanding of the language situation in the Soviet Union to examine the political institutions which were created to safeguard nationality and national language rights. These are outlined by a number of Soviet scholars whose works were translated and published in the seventies: in particular Isayev (1977), Faberov (1975) and Desheriyev (1976).

The main characteristic of the federal system of the Soviet Union is (a) that there are four different levels of federation with varying degrees of autonomy, and (b) that in the formation of these units language served as the basic criterion.

The major constituents of the USSR are the 15 *Union Republics* which are named after the majority population, have their own constitution and enjoy a maximum of autonomy, including the right to secede (at least in formal texts). In theory the majority languages of the Union Republics have the widest function: they are used at all levels of education and in all aspects of public life, though in practice the range of functions depends on the stage of linguistic development.[12] Though the 15 Union Republics formally enjoy equal rights, they vary enormously in size of territory and population, as well as in the degree of homogeneity. Nationalities other than the majority group, which occupy a contiguous territory within a Union Republic are constituted either as *Autonomous Republics, Autonomous Regions* or *National Districts*.

Within the 15 Union Republics there are 20 Autonomous Republics which likewise have their own constitution and a large degree of autonomy (legislative, administrative and cultural). In some Autonomous Republics the national language of the majority is used throughout school education, whereas smaller mother tongues are used only in primary education.

The third category is the Autonomous Regions, which consist of smaller ethnic enclaves within Union Republics. These have a statute and enjoy only administrative autonomy, though their language and education policy is supposed to follow the same principle as that of the Autonomous Republics.[13]

The smallest units are the National Districts which may be composed of one or two minority groups and are all situated in the north of the Russian Union Republic (the largest). They are granted a certain autonomy in local affairs and originally were encouraged to use their mother tongues in initial primary education. However, most members of these small groups are bilingual, either as a function of their need to communicate with other groups in the course of their daily lives, or as a result of education which switched to Russian in the forties.

Most western scholars studying the Soviet language policy praise the original Leninist concept of the principle of nationalities and support pluralist options, but concentrate on a long list of contradictions and deviations from that policy. One scholar in fact accuses Soviet Marxists of having 'imported' the western assimilationist model and claims that tsarist language policy was pluralist.[14] The counter-movement to the Leninist policy of cultural and linguistic pluralism appears to have started under Stalin, beginning with the change to the Cyrillic alphabet for all Soviet languages in the mid-1930s. In 1938 this was followed by a decree making Russian compulsory in all non-Russian schools. By the 1940s teaching in some of the small Siberian languages had stopped and a narrowing of the functions of languages below the status of the major Union Republic languages was registered. In 1958/59 there followed Krushchev's new education law which offered parents free choice to educate their children in Russian or their mother tongue, which is said to have resulted in de facto russification. However, some critics concede that the preference for education in Russian may have been a genuine choice motivated by hopes for greater social mobility.

The shift in the Soviet language policy needs to be seen in its socio-political and historical context. The pluralism of the early period was equally conditioned by the chaotic situation following the October Revolution. A centralised state apparatus had yet to be built and at every step the cooperation of the revolutionary élites of the non- Russian nationalities was needed Only later, during the period of consolidation, did the practical needs for a lingua franca become more urgent—in that context the historical advantage of Russian simply pre-empted any other choice. With the advent of World War II and the waning of the impact of revolutionary ideology, Russian nationalism crept in through the back door.

A further step on the road to Russian dominance and pressure for assimilation was the proclamation at the 22nd party congress (1961) that Russian was the 'Soviet language of inter-nationality'—a clear departure from Leninist principles. This was followed by an accelerated expansion of the teaching of Russian and a somewhat clumsy promotional campaign, while the use of other languages in administration was reduced. Brezhnev is said to have adopted the view that the nationality problem in the Soviet Union was solved and that the unity of all Soviet peoples with Russian as their common language had already been achieved.[15] Lastly, after the Tashkent Conference in 1979, a new policy was introduced to teach Russian to pre-school children and instruct parents and teachers in the methods of introducing Russian at home and in out-of-school activities—and this at a time when elsewhere in the world campaigns for mother tongue education were increasing.[16]

On the other hand, it seems that in any period the reality differed at times considerably from Soviet policy, and an increase of competence in Russian did not necessarily imply a decrease in the use and function of the national languages. Language statistics suggest that the main volume of language shift to Russian came from small linguistic groups and from individuals living outside their own national territory and hence having no access to education in their mother tongues. Of the major groups only three registered an increase in the competence of Russian accompanied by an increase in language shift (Ukrainians, Belorussians and Moldavians, the former two speaking languages closely related to Russian), whereas the populations of other Union Republics increased their competence in Russian while maintaining their mother tongues. Indeed, Union Republics with historically established languages (Georgia, Armenia, Azerbaijan, the three Baltic republics) started a counter-movement in the late seventies to preserve the purity and role of their national languages and succeeded in maintaining a clause in their constitution which defines their official state language.

Current events in the Soviet Union force us to re-examine the Soviet language policy as at least part of the wave of nationalism and separatism, which is now sweeping through the Baltic and Caucasian republics seems to be linked to what they perceive as a threat to their socio-cultural identity and language rights. To the extent that this is the case, the question which presents itself is a two-pronged one: Was the original pluralist language policy a mistake? Or is the current trouble due to its reversal to an assimilationist language policy?

To an impartial observer the positive results of the pluralist language policy are undeniable. Without strict adherence to the principle of nationalities there would have been no linguistic development of the other languages of the Soviet Union, nor could the socio-cultural awakening of the previously oppressed and underdeveloped peoples of Soviet Asia have taken place. Internal criticism inside the USSR suggests that perhaps this was too much of a good thing, or—as Soviet linguists expressed it in the seventies—the turn-about to greater emphasis on the role of Russian was justified as being a corrective measure after what they called the too-dogmatic application of Lenin's principle of full equality of languages. Lenin, however, had insisted that full equality was a *precondition* for the natural process of fusion and that this process could not be enforced, nor could one set a timetable for it. In fact, he foresaw two possible scenarios for the long-term future: either the language of a major nation would become common for all, or everyone would master three or four languages, and in neither case would the mother tongue have to be abandoned.

To a certain degree a mixture of the two scenarios was taking shape before the recent events. Minority nationalities learn the major language of the republic in which they live and usually Russian as well. Among the smallest groups language shift has increased and some languages are no longer listed in recent language censuses. Competence in Russian has enormously expanded and its dominant role as lingua franca is generally not resisted. What is resisted, however, is the infringement of Russian on linguistic rights previously granted to the major languages of the Union Republics.[17]

Also, there is resentment against Russian nationals who live in a non-Russian republic (frequently occupying top positions) while scorning to learn the local majority language. In fact Russian minorities which exist in all Union Republics have arrogated to themselves the privilege, not granted to other minorities, to have their children educated only in their mother tongue and frequently enforce Russian in the work place.

Undoubtedly, behind the policy of russification there was also a reaction to a social development familiar to us in the western world. In the stronger 'historical' nations of the Soviet Union a nationalist élite had evolved which used national sentiments and language issues for the purpose of increasing their own power. It is equally likely that some of these were corrupt. However, this does not excuse a consistent policy of replacing non-Russians in leadership positions in their own Union Republics by Russian nationals, nor the tendency to reduce non-Russian members of the Central Committee of the Communist Party and the Politbureau.[18]

Lastly, economic indicators for the five central Asian republics—Kazakhstan, Tadjikistan, Turkmenistan, Uzbekistan and Kirghizia—suggest that after seventy years of development efforts these regions still lag considerably behind the other republics.[19] While it is certainly true that ethnic conflict in the Caucasus has deep historical roots and that the democratisation process started under Gorbachev merely took the lid off the Pandora's box of nationalities, it is equally true that a great number of conflicts were exacerbated by the assimilationist policies of the last two decades, after the initial encouragement of pluralism.

What we witness in the Soviet Union is not the failure of pluralism, but the failure to consistently apply pluralist principles, be it in language policy or elsewhere. Mistakes were made at all levels—at the level of the Soviet federal government and at the level of the Union Republics and Autonomous Republics who likewise failed to respect the rights of minorities in their midst.

It is hoped that the various examples of assimilationist and pluralist language policies discussed in this chapter have helped to throw some light on the social conditions required to make such policies viable and thus to set the stage for a discussion of the options for language policies suitable for multilingual African countries.

Notes to Chapter 7

1. cf. Sankoff (1976) on precolonial relations in Papua New Guinea and the effect of the introduction of Tok Pisin and English during the period of colonialism.
2. cf. studies by Milroy (1980 and 1982), Labov (1972), and Bernstein (1971), among others.
3. cf. Leibowitz (1976).
4. cf. MacNamara (1971) and O'Cinneide (1985).
5. cf. the excellent article on diglossia in Greece by Sotiropoulos (1982) in which he analyses its social and political causes: 'The reign of Katharevousa for over 150 years represents the most logical sequence of the linguistic ideology of the ruling élite. Diglossia survived for so long because its roots were fed by the most fertile linguistic soil, that is, the social dichotomy of two separate linguistic communities within the nation.' (p.22)
6. cf. Blaut (1978: 59).
7. Blaut (1978: 148).
8. For more detail on the spread of Arabic, cf. Chejne (1969) and Rathmann et al. (1971).
9. cf. Hunt (1980), an article which contains details of a sociolinguistic survey conducted in two bilingual towns on the language border in Switzerland.
10. This section was written before the collapse of the Soviet Union. However the analysis of Soviet language policy and the conclusions drawn from the comparison of language policy and practice remain relevant and valid.
11. Lenin (1916) 'Critical Remarks on the National Question'.
12. For example, Armenian and Kirghiz are both major languages in their respective Union Republics but Kirghiz is a recently developed language and hence is or was more limited in its role.
13. An example is the Armenian enclave Nagorno Karabagh in the Union Republic of Azerbaijan where trouble started precisely because that principle was suppressed by the Azeri government. The reaction in Moscow shows that official recognition of linguistic minority rights is still, or again, seen as the best solution.
14. cf. Kreindler (1985). This was not the case and, in fact, Kreindler contradicted herself in her 1982 article by saying that in tsarist times Russian was considered as the 'cement of the Empire'. For comparison cf. Lenin's 'Lecture on the 1905 Revolution', Vol. I, p. 838 'Among the oppressed peoples of Russia there flared up a movement of national liberation. Over one half (57%) of the population of Russia is subject to national oppression; they have not even the right to use their

native language, they are forcibly russified.' cf. also Van der Planck (1978) concerning the measures taken in Russia since 1870 to enforce assimilation.

15. cf. Kreindler (1982).

16. cf. Rakowska-Harmstone (1982).

17. e.g. in the mid-1970s there was an attempt to introduce Russian as a medium of education at Tbilisi University, Georgia, and to make it compulsory for Ph.D theses to be written in Russian, after more than 50 years of using the Georgian language at university. This caused considerable disturbances.

18. Between 1952 and 1982 one third of the members of the Politbureau and the Secretariat were non-Russian (among them Uzbek, Kazakh and Azeri), whereas in 1990 there was not one Muslim representing one of the nationalities of the south in the Politbureau. The First Secretaries of the Communist Party in Azerbaijan and Kazakhstan were replaced by Russians in 1986 and 1987. cf. Ferro (1990)

19. cf. Sapir (1990) who details the discrepancy between the 1988 per capita income of the richest Union Republic (Latvia 2729 rubles) and that of the poorest (Tadjikistan 978 rubles). While this is deplorable for a socialist country, it can hardly be labeled 'colonialism'. To put this into perspective one would have to compare the per capita income of France with one of its poorest ex-colonies where the ratio is more like one to twenty.

8 Language and Nation Building in Africa

What does nation building mean in the African context and what are the roles attributed to African languages in this endeavour? To arrive at an answer to this question we must go back to African liberation movements and outline the development of the language issue in the consciousness of the African élites. The ideas concerning African languages which were expressed in the early phase of the liberation movements and those which influenced the first policy decisions after independence reveal a great deal about the nature and ideological content of African nation building. In some cases policy decisions were thought of as temporary measures, but the very fact that during the three decades of independence there has been so little change throws doubt on such an interpretation. Yet the national language issue has been kept alive by a growing number of African intellectuals outside the power cliques, and often at heavy costs to themselves. Though their ideas are frequently falsified as representing 'tribal' claims, they clearly express the conviction that pluralist solutions are the most appropriate in the multilingual African context. Some of these ideas and policies will also be examined in this chapter.

Pre-independence Liberation Movements

Characteristically for this phase the discourse of young African intellectuals was frequently inspired by Marxism and stressed the revolutionary aspect of their struggle against imperialism.[1] The title of a collection of speeches and polemic writings of Amilcar Cabral (1975) expresses their main concern very clearly: 'Unity and Struggle'. What united all Africans was their fate of being oppressed, but beyond this a great many differences loomed in the shadows, not the least of them being linguistic diversity. It is therefore little surprising that in two of his best known papers entitled 'National Liberation and Culture' and 'The Role of Culture in the Struggle for Independence' (published in the above-cited volumes) Cabral does not say a word about language, nor about the role of African languages at that time or in the future. This failure to pay attention to language problems may be explained by Nyerere's words:

> When the nationalist movements in the different countries started campaigning for independence they did not stop to argue about the ideal type of government for their country; they decided only that it was necessary to wrest sovereignty from the alien power.[2]

It seems, however, that the independence élite were generally too alienated from their African socio-cultural background to conceive an alternative to future independent statehood based on the administrative unit of the colony. Only the 'radical' members of the All-African Peoples' Conference (AAPC) stipulated that 'the independent states of Africa should amalgamate themselves into groups on the basis of geographical contiguity, economic interdependence and *linguistic and cultural affinity*' (emphasis added). It denounced 'artificial frontiers drawn by imperialist powers to divide the peoples of Africa, particularly those which cut across ethnic groups and divide people of the same stock' and called for 'the abolition or adjustment of such frontiers at an early date.'[3]

Here then we have a group of African leaders who were at least conscious of the problems involved and who were the most likely to have formulated an independent language policy. Yet the official records of the AAPC suggests that at this stage of the liberation movement language issues were not given a high priority. The resolutions of the AAPC merely call for reciprocal teaching of English and French in order to bridge the divisions created by the colonial powers, and recommended the teaching and serious study of African languages.

However, a congress organised by the Pan-African Union of Writers in 1958 in Rome called for the future adoption of a single African language for all Africa south of the Sahara. Many languages were suggested, among them: Wolof, Manding, Pulaar, Hausa, Yoruba and Swahili, but when it came to the vote the members were unable to reach a consensus. The winners in this debate were undoubtedly those African intellectuals in Paris (the 'pragmatists') who considered African languages to be an obstacle to development, and who were committed to modernisation through education in French, while making pious speeches about the preservation of African cultural values.[4]

Independence or Transfer of Power?

The majority of the élite considered independence not as a new beginning, as an opportunity for transformation or adaptation of an alien structure, but as a simple transfer of power. A well-known African film director satirised the situation as follows: black limousines drive up to the National

Assembly and from them emerge the European high functionaries of the colonial government, carrying their attaché-cases up the steps to the cabinet room where they sit down around a large table. Behind their seats stand the African high functionaries. After a signing ceremony the latter exchange places with the former and, dressed identically, carry the same attaché-cases down the steps to the same black limousines.[5] The scene from that film sums up the situation better than any words.

Statehood did not come as the result of a growing awareness of common bonds between people of different ethnic origin, nor as the result of their acknowledgment of a common destiny. The common bond which many African politicians referred to was the one created by the fact that a given territory inhabited by a number of ethnic groups was ruled by the same colonial power (generally for less than a century), creating a common administrative structure. However, it must be transparent what this meant for the people concerned. The fact of foreign domination and coercion into an alien mould can never create a true bond. The people who suffered domination, if they had hopes, their hopes must have been that it would be transitory. Independence did not always come as the result of a long protracted struggle which can create solidarity between peoples where before there was none. Many African countries were granted independence before any true mobilisation of the people had taken place—as a matter of expediency. For the colonial powers this arrangement proved to be much more beneficial than the old form of direct control, particularly as the maintenance of control was becoming too costly. In the wake of the Mau Mau uprising in Kenya, the political defeat of the Allied Suez campaign and the Algerian war of liberation both powers speedily proceeded to grant political independence, in the full knowledge that they would be able to maintain economic and ideological control.

The main tool of ideological control is language—the language chosen to be the official language and language of education. Hence the almost unanimous decision of the new African governments to maintain the languages of the former colonial powers as official languages of the new states was an important signal. Fishman (1971) interpreted this as a sign that the independence élite were primarily concerned with 'operational efficiency' rather than with authentic nationhood. Given the fact that most African countries are multilingual and had no sufficiently developed written African languages available to take over the functions of an official language, one could argue that this decision was forced upon them at the time of independence. Yet the debate has been continuing for three decades, with only a few African countries implementing a policy of linguistic self-reliance with one of their indigenous languages serving as official language in conjunction with a European language (e.g. Tanzania, Ethiopia, Somalia and Mauritania among others).

In most other countries French, English or Portuguese are still the only official languages, and the various rationalisations of the policy makers are only a thin disguise for what, in essence, amounts to self-interest. There can be no doubt that the maintenance of these languages as official languages guarantees the continuation of privileges based on the ability to manipulate these languages, and in that sense it guarantees the survival of the present élite.

Among the many examples which confirm this interpretation there is a very candid speech of the former Ugandan president Milton Obote (1967). In that speech he points out that if one of the local languages were to replace English in the Ugandan parliament, half the members would have to resign and all important positions would pass to people knowing that language, regardless of their ability and political acceptability (with the implication that knowing English makes a person both able and politically acceptable!). Furthermore, the choice of a specific language might arouse tribalism and possibly lead to civil war. He regrets the fact that, as a politician, he cannot address the people in their own language but, at the same time, is opposed to the use of Swahili, which previously was taught at school in Uganda and hence widely known. The choice of one African language over others, according to Obote, would inevitably lead to the suppression of others.

In the same vein, though expressed in the romantic metaphors of Rousseau, Leopold Senghor, ex-president of Senegal, poet and spiritual father of 'négritude' calls upon Africans (the noble savages) not to confuse nominal independence with *real* independence. Real independence is likened to a child's slow evolution into adulthood. 'We are the spiritual sons of France', says Senghor, and good Africans don't break their family ties, they merely loosen them. In the same speech (entitled 'The Will to Nationhood', 1962) made in defense of federation with Mali, he explains that 'in West Africa the fatherland is the Sérère country, the Malinké country, the Songhai country /.../ The Nation groups fatherlands in order to transcend them.'[6] While Senghor was undoubtedly right in this respect and while, for many reasons, the proposed federation could have been a step in the right direction, his main goal was to create a French commonwealth and maintain French cultural (and economic) domination.

These are two examples of African leaders defining the kind of statehood to be achieved in their countries. In their opinion the choice of an indigenous national language—often seen as the strongest bond within a nation—is either irrelevant or positively harmful. The fact that the official language was spoken only by a tiny section of the population does not appear to have worried them unduly because, in any event, the type of government they envisaged was paternalist, as had been the colonial government. Such a government requires only a minimum of downward communication, and for this purpose interpreters have proved to be adequate intermediaries. In other words: *there is no language problem*. Education in the former colonial language ensures the continuous replenishment of the ranks of the élite and serves to separate it from the masses. Meanwhile governments pay lip service to 'the heritage of our national languages' and promote their use in limited cultural or educational activities.

In response to the Pan-African movement launched by Nkrumah and the Pan-African Writers' Congress a conference was called in Monrovia in 1961, attended by representatives of countries opposed to some of the aims of the AAPC. The attendants at the Monrovia Conference represented the view that a political union of African states was premature, but that some sort of framework for cooperation should be established. As expressed in resolution 6:

> The unity that is aimed to be achieved at the moment is not the political integration of sovereign African states, but unity of aspirations and of actions considered from the point of view of African social solidarity.'[7]

Consequently the Charter of the Organization of African Unity (OAU), (founded in 1963 as the result of the Monrovia Conference) states among its principles:

> 'non-interference in the internal affairs of states' and 'respect for the sovereignty and territorial integrity of each state and for its inalienable right to independent existence.'[8]

With this the doors were closed to any form of re-organisation, revision or adjustment of borders and the colonial heritage was accepted with all the difficulties this entailed for the process of nation building which lay ahead. At the same time the new-born organisation, which had as one of its functions the peaceful settlement of disputes, was paralysed from the outset by not being endowed with tangible powers for arbitration nor any legal institution for enforcing a resolution.

Concerning language use the OAU passed only one resolution, namely to adopt English and French as its two working languages. In the field of culture and education BREDA, the African branch of UNESCO, has taken over the function of encouraging dialogue between African states in matters of education and the promotion of African languages in education. But UNESCO is bound by the same principle of non- interference and its recommendations are limited to the role that African languages should play in education. Language policy as a whole remains in the hands of the ruling élites in each African country.

The regional approach to African unity had, because of its limited scope, a greater potential for bringing about change in language policies. When in 1969 Nyerere proposed an interim solution of forming several smaller regional federations which could, eventually, be combined it was in response to the fundamental weakness of the OAU and the incompatibility of some of its member states with respect to population size, official languages, forms of administration and relationships with non-African powers. In fact Nyerere's aim was similar to that of the AAPC in 1958, only his approach was more cautious. A first step in this direction was the East African Community (EAC), founded in 1967, between Tanzania, Kenya and Uganda, essentially an economic cooperation treaty with the eventual aim of federation. As the three countries of the EAC shared a common colonial past and similar education and language policies during the colonial period (a fact which contributed considerably to the expansion and development of Swahili as the lingua franca of the entire region) the foundation of the EAC was the greatest chance in Africa for the promotion of a single African language as official language. Yet in the ten years during which the EAC functioned (1967–1977) no common language policy was adopted. While Tanzania promoted Swahili to the status of 'national language' in 1964 and to 'official language' co-equal with English in 1967, both Kenya and Uganda retained English as their sole official language, while making symbolic gestures towards Swahili.[9]

In other words: even when the conditions were as favourable as they were in East Africa, with 90% of the Tanzanian population, 65% of the Kenyan population and 35% of the Ugandan population speaking Swahili either as first or second language, the Pan-African movement presented no serious challenge to the pattern of language use as established by the colonial powers. In fact, other regional organisations such as OCAM, OMVG and OMVS tend to strengthen the role of the colonial languages in Africa and serve as a powerful counter-argument against the partisans of African official languages.

Official Language—Language of National Unity?

The concept of a pluralist society, pluralist in the cultural–linguistic sense, should not be alien to Africans since it has been a social reality in most of Africa from times immemorial. Yet what the ruling élites seem to be aiming at is the unitary model of nationhood, a model which, as we have seen, has its roots in 19th century Europe. In the absence of a common African language it is claimed that the imported official language could and would fulfil a unifying role among disparate ethnic groups and merge them into a national unit.

Presumably the concept of the 'melting pot' where language is supposed to function as the major assimilating factor was also influenced by America and other countries receiving immigrants. Yet the immigrant arriving in one of these countries finds himself in a situation of immediate contact with the language by which his assimilation is going to be measured. In most cases his voluntary move to the country of his choice prepares him mentally for cultural and linguistic adaptation. And even if the migrants themselves cannot make that jump, their children will—almost automatically—through being integrated into the education system.

In the African context we are faced with a diametrically opposed situation. The African peasant is a home in his own socio-cultural and linguistic environment and only the official language of the state he happens to live in has migrated, or rather has been imported. He has been told that the colonial rulers have departed but left their language as a gift to the new nation, and that in order to become part of this new nation—his ancestral home—he has to learn this language. He is told that this is necessary because his neighbours speak other languages, some of which he probably knows. Let us assume that our African peasant is convinced of this absurd argument and sets out in search of national integration. What happens?

In order to learn the official language African children have to attend school at least up to the Primary School Certificate, by which time they are generally supposed to have obtained a minimum acceptable level of competence in the language of instruction. In theory, at least, attendance in primary school is compulsory in most African countries, though the practice looks different. In fact, if anything, educational statistics from a few countries suggest that education in the official language is more of a barrier to integration than an aid, and thus becomes a useful tool of social control in the hands of the élite.[10]

Senegal, which had the best educational infrastructure of francophone West Africa at the time of independence, had only about 15% of its population holding a primary or higher education certificate in 1976.[11] In Sierra Leone the estimate of competent English- speakers for the same period is about 10% of the population total. This way of measuring competence in the official language—while not always accurate—provides an impression of the size of the population who are at least potentially capable of operating in that language and thus accessible to the proposed integration process. It says little about the actual use of such languages in daily life, and without daily use that process cannot even begin.

This aspect was investigated by a sociolinguistic micro survey which was carried out in Senegal in order to determine the frequency of use of French and the domains of social life in which French is used. The sample was taken from the urban educated class and the questionnaire focused on the most indicative social domains: the work place, public service agencies, family, friends, etc. The results show that the use of French among these bilinguals was essentially a function of the language requirements at work and in public places and had hardly penetrated into the private domains.[12]

A comparison with linguistic assimilation in the United States evokes a further step in that process: complete language shift. In all countries adopting a unitary language policy language shift is the ultimate goal. Where are the Africans who speak English, French or Portuguese as their mother tongue? In Guinea Bissau they are officially referred to as 'assimilados'—an estimated 0.3% of the population according to Cabral (1975), and this after 500 years of Portuguese presence. (This does not include the native speakers of Crioulo, since Creole languages are now recognised as independent languages rather than corrupt forms of a European language.) An already mentioned statistical survey from Senegal registered the Senegalese native speakers of French as 0.22% of the children enrolling in government primary schools in 1962.[13]

In view of these facts it seems that those African intellectuals who hail the coming of the Franco-African (Senghor's 'l'homme de 2000') or the approaching age of the 'Afro-Saxons' are out of touch with reality, to say the least.[14] What they display is merely the degree of their own alienation and the successful control of the African mental landscape by the colonial powers. Whether we deal with Senghor's conviction of the absolute superiority of the French language and culture and his emotional attachment to it, or Mazrui's pride in his intellectual achievement as expressed through his ability to manipulate English, the fact remains the same. As the Kenyan writer Ngugi expressed it: 'It is the final triumph of a system of domination when the dominated start singing its virtues.'[15]

Language shift is bound to remain a marginal phenomenon, even among the alienated educated élite, while the majority of Africans will continue to speak their mother tongues and learn other African languages when and where it is needed. Only a local lingua franca is likely to act as an assimilating factor and attract speakers of other languages, even to the degree of language shift.

Pluralism and the National Language Issue

The policy of promoting a single African language to the status of official language has been vociferously attacked, at times by European authors who have an interest in defending the cultural domination of Europe over Africa, but more often by Africans themselves. Such a policy has been labelled 'imperialist' and described as an attempt by certain African ethnolinguistic groups to impose their language on others in order to usurp power over the state and exclude or sideline other groups.[16] The irony here lies in the use of the word 'imperialist' referring to what amounts to official recognition of a sociolinguistic fact: namely the widespread use of a lingua franca (spoken by more than 80% of the population) while the maintenance of the foreign language spoken by at most 15% is seen as a more sensible solution.

In fact there is no contradiction between the promotion of a single African language to official status and an otherwise pluralist language policy. When Tanzania adopted Swahili as its official language it was not at the expense of the functional role of the local mother tongues but at the expense of English. Swahili is now the major language of education, public life and the urban work place, while English fulfils the purpose of an international link language and language of higher education and scientific research. Meanwhile the local mother tongues continue to play their role in traditional domains and about 90% of the Tanzanian population are bilingual (mother tongue plus Swahili). There is no evidence that Tanzanian language planners aim at creating a monolingual and monolithic society through language shift. The pattern of language use in Tanzania differs from that of its neighbouring countries only in the wider functional role of Swahili.

The practical value of this emerged before independence, in that Tanzanian politicians were able to address themselves directly to the people, without resort to interpreters, and without the distorting interference of English—the language of the same colonial power from which they wanted to free themselves. More than anything, it is this experience which gives Swahili its symbolic value as the language of Tanzanian nationhood.

Not many West African countries are in the position of having a single widespread lingua franca, but a policy similar to that in Tanzania was adopted in Mauritania. Had such a policy been implemented cautiously and wisely in Senegal, Mali and Niger in the sixties it could have produced similar results. The actual pattern of communication in those countries (cf. Chapter 5) shows that the natural trends have already created favourable conditions for making such a policy acceptable to the people—provided no political manipulation of the language issue interferes, neither from abroad nor from within the country.

Evidently there is no one solution for all cases. African countries which do not have a single lingua franca would be well advised to search for solutions more suitable to their internal sociolinguistic composition. Diversity is likely to be a feature in African countries for some time to come and the presence of a 'neutral' foreign language as official language of the state has done little to minimise the so-called 'tribal' and other cleavages where they exist. But time should have helped to deflate the myth that English, French or Portuguese would serve the goal of national integration and the creation of a national consciousness. One might argue that the Olympic Games and international football competitions have been more successful.

For some time now progressive African intellectuals have been exposing the shortcomings of their governments' language policies. 'Language alone cannot be expected to bring about national unity or to ensure the loyalty of the citizens to the state', says Kashoki (1982) in an article entitled 'Achieving Nationhood through Language'. To develop such sentiments, he demands that governments be responsive to the needs of the people, and this means, among other things, to recognise their primary loyalties. Only then will the citizens of a country begin to realise that their own personal welfare and that of their ethnic group are linked to the future of the state. In multilingual African countries integration into the national system cannot be measured by the ability to speak the official language of the state, but rather by the ability to communicate in several of its local languages, and more specifically by the range of communicative functions that the languages at a person's disposal can express.

Pluralist language policies, as we have seen in Chapter 7, are best realised in a federal system of government. Nigeria, the biggest and most heterogeneous country in West Africa, became a federation of 19 states partly in response to its colonial history and the civil war of the sixties. The boundaries of the states were redrawn several times to coincide more closely with linguistic boundaries; thus the first condition for a successful pluralist language policy seems to be fulfilled. However, despite these territorial adjustments six of the nineteen states remain highly multilingual. Since Nigeria has adopted a number of policy decision which fall into the category of a pluralist language policy, it is of particular interest in this context to examine them carefully: English has the status of official language for the whole of Nigeria and functions as such to this day. It is also the major language of education. In 1971 a declaration laid down the principle of mother tongue education in primary school, but emphasised the importance of the three major languages (Hausa, Yoruba and Ibo) and that, *in the interest of national unity,* each child should be encouraged to learn one of these three languages in addition to his own vernacular. This principle was evoked again in a decree of 1977. The constitution of 1979 also includes a proviso that these three languages are to be used in the

National House of Assembly, for the time being in addition to English, but with the long-term goal of replacing it.

State governments were empowered to determine the mother tongues and 'community languages' to be used as languages of instruction in pre-primary and primary school. They were also called upon to select other languages, in addition to Hausa, Yoruba and Ibo, to be given the special status of 'regional' or 'state' languages.[17] The remaining approximately 380 languages (61 dialect clusters according to Mann & Dalby, 1987) have the status of 'minority languages', though most of these are in fact used in the first two years of primary school. Not included in this official hierarchy of languages is Pidgin English which seems to be gaining ground as unofficial lingua franca and is even claimed to be developing into a Creole (i.e. that it has a mother tongue community).

A further boost to the status of the three major languages was the policy that state governments should select one or two Nigerian languages (in addition to English) for the purpose of conducting state business in the House of Assembly. In 1983 seven of the nineteen states chose Hausa for this purpose, four chose Yoruba, two chose Ibo and six opted for English only.

One of the critics of the Nigerian language policy points out that its goals are inconsistent and contradictory and that 'the threat to nationalism is not so much from the large number of indigenous languages as from English.'[18] The most hotly debated federal policy decisions, which have in fact not been implemented (it is claimed because of lack of teachers) concern the status and role of the three major languages. One evidently biased and short-sighted commentator shall serve as an example to demonstrate how easy it is to whip up emotional responses to language issues. He writes:

> In Plateau State there are about 70 different languages, though Hausa has rendered them 'bedroom' languages or undeveloped languages. The situation in Plateau State today is that of a multilingual environment that has degenerated into diglossia.'[19]

He further mentions that Benue State 'has been able to resist the incursion of Hausa', as if this were some kind of moral victory. The writer also claims that Nigerian languages are 'tribe-bound' (though he acknowledges the widespread use of Hausa, Yoruba and Ibo as lingua francas), that none of the speakers of the three major languages would be willing to learn another language and that English should remain the national language.

In reply to the phrases quoted it needs to be emphasised that, firstly, diglossia is not a state of degeneration, but a sociolinguistic pattern found, to some degree in all multilingual, but also in monolingual countries. The use of English as official language (which the above author recommends) exemplifies one variety of a diglossic situation. Secondly, it is not the Hausa language which rendered the others 'bedroom languages'; it was social change which transformed the previously isolated small linguistic communities and integrated them into a larger unit. Such a context requires the use of a lingua franca for the purposes of inter-ethnic communication, while mother tongues are maintained in the family domain and traditional social relations. Lingua francas are not imposed: they are generally adopted voluntarily, and the choice of a lingua franca is determined by its usefulness as a vehicle for wider communication. This form of diglossia is extremely common and no social stigma should be attached to the fact that a person's mother tongue is a small minority language. While it is true that such languages usually remain undeveloped, because the lingua franca tends to take over the domains where modernisation and vocabulary extension would occur, this has been the fate of almost all languages spoken by small groups since the beginning of time, particularly during periods of transition.

Thirdly, discussions about language policy concern the role which a language or languages should play in public life; in other words we are dealing with the instrumental aspect of language, not with sociolinguistic identity or the cultural values and resources of a language. Thus the only valid argument against using a particular language in public life is its insufficient spread. Therefore, when the state governments of the Nigerian federation were called upon to select a Nigerian language for use in their House of Assembly, and presumably in other government agencies, the internal language situation should have been the most appropriate guide. The question should have been: is there a widespread lingua franca or a majority language in our state (or in a neighbouring state) which may assume this role, or which may be developed and encouraged to assume this role? And if so, by what means can the speakers of other languages be assured that they will not be disadvantaged?

There does, indeed, seem to be confusion and contradiction in the wording of the Nigerian language policy. For while furthering the spread of the three major lingua francas and encouraging their use, the emotional–integrative appeal to 'national unity' is somewhat out of place. The best that these three languages can be expected to do in the context of Nigeria is to act as a bond within those regions where these languages are influential and to facilitate communication between the states as well as between the states and the federal government. The principle of reciprocal language learning in order to create mutual understanding between the diverse groups of Nigeria is also likely to arouse negative reactions as long as it is applied only to some languages and not to others.

Lastly, it is not enough to have a federal structure and to adjust some of the state boundaries to correspond more closely to linguistic boundaries. The role of a certain number of languages must be territorially defined; and in Nigeria this would involve several levels of organisation, as in the Soviet Union, in order to create 'security zones' for smaller language communities. Switzerland selected two of its four languages as working languages at the federal level, and in Nigeria the three chosen major languages are appropriate for this purpose for the majority of the states. However, before such a policy can be applied for communication between the federal government and the six other states where these languages are not sufficiently known, measures would have to be taken to provide special training courses for civil servants, translation services and every possible incentive to make such a change attractive.

The major problem with Nigeria's language policy, as indeed with language policy in Africa in general, is that policy decisions tend to be taken arbitrarily. No national sociolinguistic surveys were carried out in West Africa before or after policy formulation. The statistics concerning the size of mother tongue communities vary considerably from the point of view of reliability; reliable statistics on the population speaking a lingua franca as second language are non-existent (we usually have to contend ourselves with estimates), and no evaluation was made of what the implementation of the language policy would entail. However, Nigeria appears to be fertile ground for ideas concerning language policy and practice, and though workable solutions may not be around the corner, the need for them is openly discussed.[20]

Other types of pluralist solutions may be sought in the frame of larger regional configurations, such as the already mentioned East African Community which consisted of Tanzania, Kenya and Uganda (cf. above) or the federation between Senegal and Mali, as envisaged by Senghor, or indeed the confederation between Senegal and Gambia which was inaugurated in the early eighties, or any of the regional organisations which sprung up around a common economic interest, such as the development and use of water resources. For instance, the two organisations grouping the countries which share the Gambia and Senegal rivers (OMVG and OMVS) have two lingua francas at their disposal which are shared by most of their member countries: *Manding*, the major lingua franca of Mali, also spoken in Guinea, Guinea Bissau, Senegal and Gambia; and *Wolof*, spoken in Senegal, Mauritania, Gambia, and to a limited extent also in Mali. However, the tradition of using interpreters in meetings between officials of anglophone and francophone countries is so entrenched that it requires a technical break-down to make people realise that they can very well communicate with their counterparts in an African lingua franca.[21] The use of African lingua francas in the larger, regional context could, further-more, defuse some of the tensions and hostilities evoked by status change within the national frame, and with time establish patterns which may then become acceptable at the national level as well.

Conclusion: The Goals of Language Planning

Nation building and language planning are two modern concepts which clearly express the deliberate, even mechanistic character of these activities and their utilitarian goal. A nation which can be built must be different from one which was thought of as something organic, possessing as its life blood a common language (cf. the 19th century Herder model).

Indeed, in the modern context a nation might be more appropriately compared to a multi-storey building housing many families, and in order for these to be able to live in peace it is necessary to lay down the ground rules for their interaction. This is the function of political and social institutions to which all members of the community must have equal access. Part of the establishment of a communal house therefore involves the creation of a system of communication which will enable the institutions to function effectively and equitably. This should be the sole concern of language planning and, above all, language planning should not be confused with social engineering, with methods introducing social change from above. The deliberate manipulation of language/s for the purpose of eliminating regional differences, for 'national integration' into a monolithic society, is likely to be counter-productive.

Language planning is a rather delicate tool which, in the hands of specialists, may produce results beneficial to society. It is an interdepend-ent set of procedures which involve different kinds of specialists and which must be carried out in a certain sequence. Formulating a language policy is part of this procedure but, contrary to current practice in Africa, it is not or should not be the first step. A policy decision taken without prior sociolinguistic surveys and their scientific analysis is likely to be arbitrary, and no amount of subsequent efforts can save it from failure.

Furthermore, language policy decisions should fit into a framework of larger social goals for which a consensus has been reached. The more technical aspects of language planning (devising a writing system, formu-lating grammatical rules, compiling dictionaries, modernising the vocabu-lary through borrowing and coining, etc.) are less likely to be problematical because these are the undisputed province of language specialists. Political motivations may once again enter the field at the level of promotion, evaluation and implementation and distort the results. In other words, the outcome of language planning can never be guaranteed to correspond to the initially stated goal. Its failure is a *political failure*, related to the unwillingness of the ruling class to recognise ethnolinguistic groups as legitimate interest groups whose conflicting demands must be solved by negotiation, arbitration and compromise.

The commonly held view that in multilingual countries there is an *inherently harmful* dichotomy between primordial group loyalty (called 'tribalism' when referring to Africa) and civic loyalty to the state betrays a fundamentally authoritarian interpretation of political processes. Such different loyalties are not necessarily mutually contradictory, and in many European nations a tolerant attitude towards diversity has encouraged the development of a bifocal process of identification (which, in fact, runs parallel to the twin functions of language discussed in Chapter 7).

One focus is the profoundly symbolic, emotional identification with one's place of origin and its dialect or language; the other a more rational, conscious form of attachment to the state and its official language. Both relations involve rights and obligations, but whereas the former is bound up with the unconscious part of personal identity and hence not negotiable, civic loyalty to the state generally develops as a conscious moral commitment, or it may come partly as a response to tangible rewards. In a situation where a blatantly unjust and corrupt regime blocks any kind of moral commitment, or where the individual is made to feel excluded from the reward system, he has only two options: either to fall back on his primordial loyalty group, become a regional activist and potential secessionist, or to migrate to another region and possibly to another country.

The Scots are a good example for this type of sociolinguistic behaviour. They identify strongly with their region and signal this with a distinct variety of English, but generally they are ready to accept their civic duties towards Great Britain. However, unequal treatment of Scotland by the British government from time to time provokes protest and demands for greater autonomy. Also, the migration ratio among the Scots used to be a lot higher than that of British citizens as a whole, and the same applies to an even larger degree to the Irish.

In theory this type of bifocal identification should be equally possible in African countries, even though ethnolinguistic diversity is quantitatively higher and linguistic distance between neighbouring languages may be greater. By observing the linguistic behaviour of many small and medium size ethnolinguistic groups it becomes clear that their members have no difficulty in recognising the advantage of being incorporated into a larger unit and that they respond to this situation by becoming bilingual or polyglot. In such contexts language learning is seen as a worthwhile investment since it opens up new opportunities for social mobility. However, it would be hypocritical to pretend that demographic factors are of no importance in language politics, and the example of Nigeria bears witness to this. Nigeria has not only a multitude of small ethnolinguistic groups; its three major linguistic groups are each of the size of a medium-size nation in Europe and approximate the population of Senegal, Mali and Guinea taken together.[22] The Nigerian case would benefit from a comparison with the negotiations in the European Parliament concerning minority language rights and the role of the working languages of the EEC.

Unfortunately, the sociolinguistic situation in African countries is fundamentally different for reasons of their economic dependence and internal political situation. The majority of African countries are governed by military juntas or single parties headed by authoritarian rulers, in some cases the same person for twenty or thirty years. Invariably these have succeeded in cementing their hold on power by surrounding themselves with members of their clan and filling important positions with loyal supporters from their ethnic group or region of origin. It should therefore be of little surprise that any language planning activity concerning African languages is viewed with suspicion as a further move to exclude others from power.

On the whole, though, both language planning and nation building are more frequently alluded to in speeches than put into practice, for both are instruments of a democratic society. There are those who hold the view that democratic processes are not suitable for periods of social and economic transition, that economic development is the first priority and that it is best served by authoritarian governments. However, after thirty years of concerted efforts at development—as defined by outside powers—the negative results clearly show that once again Africa has been cheated. The last decade of this century may well see the second decolonisation of Africa, and an integral part of such an effort should be the 'decolonisation of the mind'.[23]

Notes to Chapter 8

1. cf. Kwame Nkrumah, ex-president of Ghana: 'Towards African Unity' in Mutiso & Rohio (1975).
2. Julius Nyerere: 'United States of Africa' in Mutiso & Rohio (1975).
3. All-African Peoples Conference (1958) Resolutions, in Mutiso & Rohio (1975: 360). The AAPC represented Ghana, Egypt, Sudan, Libya, Tunisia, Morocco, Ethiopia and Liberia and was centered around the presidents Nkrumah and Nasser.
4. cf. Alexandre (1963).
5. The film is called 'Xaala', directed by the Senegalese Sembène Ousmane.
6. Leopold Senghor 'The Will to Nationhood' in: Mutiso & Rohio (1975: 584).

7. Mutiso & Rohio (1975: 392).
8. Mutiso & Rohio (1975: 394).
9. Kenya's Bantu population amounts to 63% of the population total (for these Swahili is easy to learn, because related). 65% of the Kenyan population speak Swahili either as mother tongue or as second language, and rural samples show a higher proportion of Swahili speakers. Yet a move to promote Swahili to official language failed in 1970. Swahili was given the status of 'national language' in 1974, with the only practical change that it became accepted in parliamentary debates—a move which has been described as one of Kenyatta's election stunts to appease the partisans of Swahili. Uganda has a Bantu population of 65% and 35% speak Swahili which had always been the lingua franca of the army and police. President Idi Amin promoted Swahili to the status of 'national language', while English was to remain temporarily the official language. Again no practical steps were taken to introduce change.
10. cf. the following education statistics taken from *Africa South of the Sahara* (1990): *Senegal* (medium of education French): enrolment in primary school: 53% of age-group 6–12; secondary school enrolment: 13% of age-group 12–18 (in 1985); *Sierra Leone* (medium of education English): enrolment in primary school: 58% of age group 5– 12; secondary school: 17% of age-group 12–18 (in 1982); *Guinea Bissau* (medium of education Portuguese) enrolment in primary school: 53% of age-group 7–13; secondary school: 3% of age-group 13–18 (in 1983/84).
11. cf. the 1976 census: the statistics for the level of education in 3 country districts (Casamance, Thies, Diourbel) refer to 12.77% of the population holding the primary school certificate, of which a further 2.13% had completed further education. cf. also Blonde (1975) and Dalby (1978).
12. The following is an extract from Blonde (1975): *Work Place*: 33% of the sample always use French, 47% very often, 17.5% sometimes, 2.5% never; *In public places* (post office, bank etc.): 40% always, 27.5% very often, 27% sometimes, 6.5% never; *In the family*: 3% always, 17% very often, 52.5% sometimes, 28% never; *Among friends* (outside the home) : 7.5 % always, 29% very often, 51% sometimes, 12.5% never.
13. cf. Wioland (1965) The number of French-speaking children would be slightly higher if children entering a small number of private schools had been encluded.
14. Mazrui (1975) predicts that by the year 2000 there will be more 'Afro-Saxons' (i.e. African, American and Caribbean native speakers of English) than inhabitants of the British Isles.
15. Ngugi Wa Thiong'o (1986: 20).
16. cf. Apter (1982). Also the classical response of the Senegalese President, Abdou Diouf, when interviewed on the topic of cultural authenticity and whether it wasn't time to recognise Wolof as the official national language of Senegal: 'Il faut craindre de remplacer un imperialisme par un autre' (Le Soleil, 24/25 April 1982).
17. i.e. Fulani, Efik, Kanuri, Tiv, Ijo, Edo, Nupe, Igala and Idoma.
18. cf. Akinnaso (1989).
19. cf. Fakuade (1989: 57).
20. cf. also Bamgbose (1989) and a recent suggestion to create an artificial language, a kind of compound of elements of all Nigerian languages called 'Guosa' which

would provide a common vehicle of communication while at the same time being specifically Nigerian (Note in Language Problems and Language Planning 12 (3), 277).

21. An anecdote circulated in Dakar among interpreters about a conference of Senegalese and Gambian ministers which suddenly found itself without interpretation service and, after a moments hesitation, it was ascertained that everyone present was fluent in Wolof, and the meeting proceeded in Wolof. On another occasion I witnessed how the Director of an international research team sent to Guinea, a native speaker of Manding from northern Mali, was able to establish personal contact through the use of Manding with Guinean officials in most provinces. Similar incidents are reported by Treffgarne (1975).

22. There are approximately 22 million native speakers of Hausa, 20 million native speakers of Yoruba and 17 million native speakers of Ibo, and these figures exclude the millions of second language speakers.

23. Ngugi Wa Thiong'o (1986: 20).

References

ADAMS, A. 1987, La force subversive des langues africaines. *Le Monde Diplo-matique*, August.

AKINNASO, F.N. 1989, One nation, four hundred languages: Unity and diversity in Nigeria's language policy. *Language Problems and Language Planning* 13 (2).

ALEXANDRE, P. 1963, Les problèmes linguistiques africaines vus de Paris. In J. SPENCER (ed) *Language in Africa*. Cambridge: Cambridge University Press.

— 1967, *An Introduction to Languages and Language in Africa* (English Translation, 1972). London: Heinemann.

AMIN, S. 1974, Introduction. In S. AMIN and D. FORDE (eds) *Modern Migrations in Western Africa*. London: Oxford University Press.

APTER, A.H. 1982, National language planning in plural societies: The search for a framework. *Language Problems and Language Planning* 12 (3).

ATLAS DU SENEGAL 1977, Paris: Institut Géographique Nationale.

BAMGBOSE, A. 1989, Issues for a model of language planning. *Language Problems and Language Planning* 13 (1).

BERNSTEIN, B. 1971, *Class, Codes and Control*. London: Routledge & Kegan Paul.

BESSIS, S. 1989, Le Sénégal, la Mauritanie et leurs boucs émissaires. *Le Monde Diplomatique*, July 1990.

BINGER, L.G. 1892, *Du Niger au Golfe de Guinee*. Paris.

BIRD, C. 1970, The development of Mandekan. In D. DALBY (ed.) *Language and History in Africa*. London: Cass & Co.

BLAUT, J. 1978, *The National Question*. London: Zed Books.

BLONDE, J. 1975, *Analyse des résultats d'un premier essai de sondage sociolinguistique effectué en milieu lettré*. Dakar: CLAD

BOADI, L. 1976, Mother tongue education in Ghana. In A.BAMGBOSE (ed.) *Mother Tongue Education: The West African Experience*. London: Hodder & Stoughton.

BOAHEN, A.A. (ed) 1985 *General History of Africa. Vol VII: Africa under Colonial Domination 1880–1935*. Paris: UNESCO.

BOCANDE, B. 1849, Notes sur la Guinée Portugaise ou Sénégambie méridionale. *Bulletin de la Societé de Géographie*. Paris.

BROOKS, G. 1980, Kola trade and state-building: Upper Guinea Coast and Sene-gambia, 15-17th centuries. Boston University Working Papers, No.38 (African Studies).

CABRAL, A. 1975, *Unité et lutte. Vol.I*. Paris: Maspero.

CALVET, M. and WIOLAND, F. 1967, *L'expansion du Wolof au Sénégal*. Dakar: CLAD

CALVET, L.-J. 1981, *Les Langues Véhiculaires*. Paris: Presses Universitaires.

— 1982, The spread of Mandingo: Military, commercial and colonial influence on a linguistic datum. In R.L. COOPER (ed.) *Language Spread*. Bloomington, IN: Indiana University Press.

— 1987, *La Guerre des Languages et Les Politiques Linguistiques*. Paris: Payot.

CECCALDI, P. 1974, *Essai de nomenclature des populations, languages et dialectes de Côte d'Ivoire*. Paris: CARDAN.

CHEJNE, A. 1969, *The Arabic Language in History*. Minneapolis: University of Minneapolis Press.

CROWDER, M. 1968, *West Africa under Colonial Rule*. London: Hutchinson & Co.

DALBY, D. 1969, Major languages of Sierra Leone. In J.I. CLARKE (ed.) *Sierra Leone in Maps*. London: University of London Press.

— (ed.) 1970, *Language and History in Africa*. New York: Africana Publishing Corporation.

— 1971, Distribution and nomenclature of the Manding People and their language. In C.T. HODGE (ed.) *Papers on the Manding*. The Hague: Mouton.

— 1978, *Language Map of Africa*. London: International African Institute.

DELAFOSSE, M. 1913, Traditions historiques et légendaires du Soudan Occidentale (translation of a manuscript in Arabic). Paris: Publication du Comité de l'Afrique Française.

DESHERIYEV, Y. 1976, A case in point: The Soviet experience with languages. *Prospects* VI (3). Paris: UNESCO.

DJITE, P.G. 1988a, Correcting errors in language classification: Monolingual nuclei and multilingual satellites. *Language Problems and Language Planning* 12 (1).

— 1988b, The spread of Dyula and popular French in Côte d'Ivoire: Implications for language policy. *Language Problems and Language Planning* 12 (3).

DOKE, C.M. 1967, *The Southern Bantu Languages*. London: Dawsons.

DONEUX, J.L. 1977, Les langues du Sénégal. In *Atlas National du Sénégal*. Paris: Institut Géographique National.

— 1978, Les liens historiques entre les langues du Sénégal. *Réalités Africaines et Langue Française*. Dakar: CLAD.

FABEROV, N.P. 1975, Self-determination in the Soviet Union. In W. MACKEY and A. VERDOODT (eds) *The Multinational Society*. Rowley, Mass.: Newbury House.

FAGE, J.D. 1969, *A History of West Africa*. London: Cambridge University Press.

FAGE, J.D. and VERITY, M. (eds) 1978, *An Atlas of African History*. New York: Africana Publishing Corporation.

FAKUADE, G. 1989, A three-language formula for Nigeria: Problems of implementation. *Language Problems and Language Planning* 13 (1).

FERGUSON, C.A. 1971, National Sociolinguistic Profile formula. In C.A. FERGUSON (ed.) *Language Structure and Language Use*. Stanford: Stanford University Press.

FERRO, M. 1990, Des républiques à la dérive. *Le Monde Diplomatique* May.

FISHMAN J.A. 1971, National languages and languages of wider communication. In W.H. WHITELEY (ed.) *Language Use and Social Change*. London: Oxford University Press.

FISHMAN, J.A. 1972, *Language and Nationalism*. Rowley, Mass: Newbury House Publishers.

GIGLIOLI, P.P. (ed.) *Language and Social Context*. London: Penguin.

GNIELINSKI,S. Von (ed.) 1972, *Liberia in Maps*. London: University of London Press.

GOODY. J. 1964, The Mande and the Akan hinterland. In J.VANSINA, J.R. MAUNY and L.V. THOMAS (eds) *The Historian in Tropical Africa*. London: Oxford University Press.

GOODY, J. and WATT, I. 1972, The consequences of literacy. In P.P. GIGLIOLI (ed.) *Language and Social Context*. London: Penguin.

GREENBERG, J.H. 1963, *The Languages of Africa*. The Hague: Mouton.

GRIFFETH, R.R. 1971, The Dyula impact on the peoples of the West Volta region. In C.T. HODGE (ed.) *Papers on the Manding*. The Hague: Mouton.

HAIR, P.E.H. 1966, The use of African languages in Afro-European contacts in Guinea: 1440–1560. *Sierra Leone Language Review* V (10).

HEINE, B. 1970, *Status and Use of African Lingua Francas*. München: Weltforum Verlag.

HODGE, C.T. (ed) 1971, *Papers on the Manding*. The Hague: Mouton.

HOUIS, M. 1959, Le groupe linguistique Mandé. *Notes Africaines* No.82

HUNT, J.A. 1980, Education and bilingualism on the language frontier in Switzerland. *Journal of Multilingual and Multicultural Development* 1 (1).

INGLEHART, R.F. and WOODWARD, M. 1972, Language conflicts and political community. In P.P. GIGLIOLI (ed.) *Language and Social Context*. London: Penguin.

ISAYEV, M.I. 1977, *National Languages in the USSR : Problems and Solutions*. Moscow: Progress Publishers.

KASHOKI, M.E. 1982, Achieving nationhood through language: The challenge of Namibia. *Third World Quarterly* 4 (2).

KREINDLER, I. 1982, The changing status of Russian in the Soviet Union. *International Journal of the Sociology of Language* 33.

— 1985, *Sociolinguistic Perspectives on Soviet National Languages*. Berlin: Mouton de Gruyter.

LABOV, W. 1972, *Language in the Inner Cities: Studies in the Black English Vernacular*. Philadelphia: University of Pennsylvania Press.

LADEFOGED, P.R., GLICK, R. and CRIPER, C. (eds) 1972, *Language in Uganda*. Nairobi: Oxford University Press.

LEIBOWITZ, A.H. 1976, Language and the law: The exercise of political power. In W.M. and J.F. O'BARR (eds) *Language and Politics*. The Hague: Mouton.

LENIN, V.I. 1916, *Critical Remarks on the National Question*. Moscow: Foreign Languages Publishing House (1954).

LEVTZION, N. and J.F.P.HOPKINS (eds) 1981, *Corpus of Early Arabic Sources for West African History*. Cambridge: Cambridge University Press.

LEWIS, B. 1971, The Dioula in the Ivory Coast. In C.T. HODGE (ed.) *Papers on the Manding*. The Hague: Mouton.

LLOYD, P.C. 1970, The ethnic background to the Nigerian crisis. In S.K.PANTER-BRICK (ed.) *Nigerian Politics and Military Rule: Prelude to the Civil War*. London: Athlone Press.

LY-TALL, M. 1977, *Contribution à l'histoire de l'Empire du Mali*. Dakar: Nouvelles Editions Africaines.

— 1984, The decline of the Mali empire. In D.T. NIANE (ed.) *General History of Africa. Vol. IV: Africa from the Twelfth to the Sixteenth Century*. Paris: UNESCO

M'BAYE GUEYE and A. A. BOAHEN 1985, African initiatives and resistance in West Africa, 1880–1914. In A. A. BOAHEN (ed.) *General History of Africa. Vol. VII: Africa Under Colonial Domination, 1880–1935*. Paris: UNESCO.

MACNAMARA, J. 1971, Success and failures in the movement for the restoration of Irish. In J.RUBIN and B. JERNUDD (eds) *Can Language Be Planned?* Honolulu: University Press of Hawaii.

MANN, M. and DALBY, D. 1987, *A Thesaurus of African Languages*. London: International African Institute.

MANSOUR, G. 1980, The dynamics of multilingualism: The case of Senegal. *Journal of Multilingual and Multicultural Development* 1 (4).

MAZRUI, A. 1975, *The Political Sociology of the English Language*. The Hague: Mouton.

McCALL, D. 1971, The cultural map and time profile of the Mande-speaking peoples. In C.T.HODGE (ed.) *Papers on the Manding*. The Hague: Mouton.

MILROY, L. 1980, *Language and Social Networks*. Oxford: Basil Blackwell.

— 1982, Language and group identity. *Journal of Multilingual and Multicultural Development* 3 (3).

MOLLIEN, M. 1820, *Voyage dans l'interieur de l'Afrique aux sources du Sénégal et de la Gambie, 1818*. Paris: Imprimerie Veuve Courcier.

MUTISO, G.-C.M. and ROHIO, S.W. (eds) 1975, *Readings in African Political Thought*. London: Heinemann.

NGUGI WA THIONG'O 1986, *Decolonizing the Mind*. London: James Currey.

NIANE, D.T. 1960, *Soundjata ou l'épopée mandingue*. Paris: Présence Africaine.

— 1975, *Recherches sur l'Empire du Mali au Moyen Age*. Paris: Présence Africaine.

— 1984a, Mali and the second Mandingo expansion. In D.T. NIANE (ed.) *General History of Africa, Vol. IV: Africa from the Twelfth to the Sixteenth Century*. Paris: UNESCO.

— (ed.) 1984b, *General History of Africa. Vol. IV: Africa from the Twelfth to the Sixteenth Century*. Paris: UNESCO.

NIDA, E.A. and WONDERLY, W. 1971, Communication roles of languages in multilingual societies. In W.H. WHITELEY (ed.) *Language and Social Change*. London: Oxford University Press.

NKRUMAH, K. 1958, Towards African Unity. In G. MUTISO and S.W. ROHIO (eds) *Readings in African Political Thought*. London: Heinemann.

NOLAN, R.W. 1977, L'histoire des migrations bassari influences et perspectives. *Journal des Africanistes* 42 (2).

NYERERE, J.K. 1968, The united states of Africa. In G. MUTISO and W.S. ROHIO (eds) *Readings in African Political Thought*. London: Heinemann.

O'CINNEIDE, M.S. *et al.* 1985, Industrialization and linguistic change among Gaelic-speaking communities in the West of Ireland. *Language Problems and Language Planning* 9 (1).

OBOTE, M. 1967, *Language and National Identification*. East Africa Journal, April.

OHANNESSIAN, S. and KASHOKI, M.E. (eds) 1978, *Language in Zambia*. London: International African Institute.

OSAJI B. 1979, *Language Survey in Nigeria*. Quebec: International Center for Research on Bilingualism.

PARK, M. 1799, *Travels in the Interior Districts of Africa*. (reprinted 1969). London: Everyman's Library.

PARKIN, D. 1971, Language choice in two Kampala housing estates. In W.H. WHITELEY (ed.) *Language Use and Social Change*. Oxford: Oxford University Press.

PERSON, Y. 1964, Enquête d'une chronologie ivorienne. In J. VANSINA, R. MAUNY and L.V. THOMAS (eds) *The Historian in Tropical Africa*. London: Oxford University Press.

— 1971, Ethnic movements and acculturation in Upper Guinea since the 15th century. *African Historical Studies* 4 (3).

— 1984, The coastal peoples: From Casamance to the Ivory Coast lagoons. In D.T. NIANE (ed.) *General History of Africa, Vol. IV: Africa from the Twelfth to the Sixteenth Century*. Paris: UNESCO.

PESHKIN, A. 1967, Education and national integration in Nigeria. *Journal of Modern African Studies*. 5 (3).

POOL, J. 1969, National development and language diversity. *La Monda Lingvo-Problema* 1.

QUINN, C. 1972, *Mandingo Kingdoms of the Senegambia*. London: Longmans.

RAKOWSKA-HARMSTONE, T. 1982, A political perspective. *International Journal of the Sociology of Language* 33.

RATHMANN, L. (ed) 1971, *Geschichte der Araber*. Berlin: Akademie Verlag.

ROCHE, C. 1976, *Conquête et résistance des peuples de Casamance*. Dakar: Nouvelle Editions Africaines.

RODNEY, W. 1975, The Guinea Coast. In R. GRAY (ed.) *The Cambridge History of Africa. Vol.4*. Cambridge: Cambridge University Press.

SANKOFF, G. 1976, Political power and linguistic inequality in Papua New Guinea. In W.M. and J.F. O'BARR (eds) *Language and Politics*. The Hague: Mouton.

SAPIR, J. 1990, Un 'Sud' a l'abandon. *Le Monde Diplomatique* May.

SAPIR, J.D. 1965, *A Grammar of Diola-Fogny*. Cambridge: Cambridge University Press.

SCOTTON, C.M. 1980, Review article of S.OHANNESSIAN and M.E. KASHOKI. *Journal of African Languages and Linguistics* 2.

— 1982a, Language use in Kenya: An urban-rural comparison of the Luyia. *International Journal of the Sociology of Language* 34.

— 1982b, Learning lingua francas and socio-economic integration. In R.L. COOPER (ed.) *Language Spread*. Indiana: Indiana University Press.

SENGHOR, L.S. 1962, The will to nationhood. In G. MUTISO and S.W. ROHIO (eds) *Readings in African Political Thought*. London: Heinemann.

SOTIROPOULOS, D. 1982, The social roots of modern Greek diglossia. *Language Problems and Language Planning* 6 (1).

SOW, A.I. (ed) 1977, *Langues et Politiques de Langues en Afrique Noire*. Paris: UNESCO.

STEVENS, P. 1983, Ambivalence, modernisation and language attitudes: French and Arabic in Tunisia. *Journal of Multilingual and Multicultural Development* 4 (2-3).

SUNDSTROM, L. 1974, *The Exchange Economy of Precolonial Tropical Africa*. London: Hurst & Co.

SURET-CANALE, J. 1973, *Afrique Noire Occidentale et Centrale*. Paris: Editions Sociales.

TABOURET-KELLER, A. 1971, Language use in relation to the growth of towns in West Africa. *International Migration Review* 5 (2).

TEIXEIRA DA MOTA, A. 1978, *Some Aspects of Portuguese Colonisation and Sea Trade in West Africa in the 15th and 16th centuries*. Bloomington: Indiana University African Studies Program.

TREFFGARNE, C. 1975, *The Role of English and French as Languages of Communication between Anglophone and Francophone West African States*. London: Africa Educational Trust.

UNESCO 1982, (unpublished) *Survey of Community Languages*.

UZOIGWE, G.N. 1985, European partition and conquest of Africa. In A. A. BOAHEN (ed) *General History of Africa, Vol. VII: Africa under Colonial Domination, 1880–1935*. Paris: UNESCO.

VAN DER PLANK, P.H. 1978, The assimilation and non-assimilation of European linguistic minorities. In J.A. FISHMAN (ed.) *Advances in the Study of Societal Multilingualism*. The Hague: Mouton.

VANSINA, J., MAUNY, R. and THOMAS, L.V. (eds) 1964 *The Historian in Tropical Africa*. London: Oxford University Press.

WHELMERS, W.E. 1971, Niger-Congo, Mande. In T. SEBEOK (ed.) *Current Trends in Linguistics*. Vol. 7. The Hague: Mouton.

WHITELEY, W.H. (ed) 1971, *Language Use and Social Change*. London: Oxford University Press.

WILKS, I. 1962, A medieval trade-route from the Niger to the Gulf of Guinea. *Journal of African History* 3 (2).

WIOLAND, F. 1965, *Enquête sur les langues parlées au Sénégal*. Dakar: CLAD

WRIGHT, D.R. 1977, Darbo Jula: The role of a Mandinka Jula clan in the long distance trade of the Gambia river and its hinterland. *African Economic History* No.3, Spring.

Index

Adult literacy 87
African languages
— as official language 123
— classification of 14
— in the media 87
— rehabilitation of 81
— status of 11
African lingua franca, regional 130
African linguistics 11, 12
Akan languages 70
Arab sources 33, 43, 52
Arabic
— as official language 92, 107
— expansion of 108
— use of 34
Arabisation of education 93
Assimilation 102, 113
— and conversion 108
— and language shift 41
— and linguistic unification 98
— social process of 19
— the case of Arabic 107
Assimilationist language policies 103, 115
Autonomous village societies 45, 49

Berlin Conference 65
Bilingual societies 5
Bilingualism 7, 103, 110

Coastal cities, sociolinguistic development in 62
Colonial rule 51, 58, 59
Colonialism, heritage of 24
Communication
— barriers to 45
— system of 3
Communicative functions 127
Community languages 75
Contact languages 37

Contact situations 5
Creole
— communities 64
— languages 76, 77, 82, 101
Creolised languages: French, English or Portuguese 62
Crioulo 54, 125

Dialect 14
— cluster 26, 70
— continuum 68
— variation 13
Diglossia 104, 128
Domain cluster
— primary 85
— secondary 85
Domains 20, 84, 126

East African community 123, 130
Education and literacy, multilingual context of 84
Educational policy, African languages 78
Empire of Ghana 28, 31, 37
Empire of Mali 28, 36, 56
Ethnic minorities 24
Ethnic strife 96
Ethno-linguistic boundaries 97
European trading stations 61
Extra-linguistic factors 28

Fragmentation, language divergence 47
French
— as language of public communication 59
— commonwealth 121
— frequency of use of 124
French West Africa 65
Function of language, 73, 75, 102

Functional specialisation of languages
   86
Functions of communication
— in group 20
— out-group 20
— specialised 20

Gabu 56
Guinea Coast 38, 46

Hausa 94, 97, 127
Hierarchy of languages 101, 128
Horizontal multilingualism 46

Ibo 94, 127
Independence 119–121
Indirect rule, Nigeria 95
Inter-ethnic communication 16, 73
Inter-intelligibility 50

Joola 47, 50
— communities 49
— social and linguistic fragmentation
   51
— splinter languages 47
Jula 35, 64
— trade route 39, 52

Krio 63

Labour migrations 60
Language
— and dialect 2
— and education policy 112
— and nation 1, 104, 118
— and society 4
— behaviour, social rule of 50
— cultural identity 41
— expansion 23, 54
— fragmentation 23
— functional allocation of 15
— issues 97, 98, 115, 118
        and the Nigerian Civil War 94
— labels 12, 13
— of education 120
— planning 92, 131, 133
— policy 21, 78, 92–94, 97, 102, 119, 123
    – colonial 77
    – in the Soviet Union 111
    – Nigerian 128, 129, 130
    – Soviet 114

— rights 110, 112, 114
— shift 7, 13, 19, 35, 37–39, 47, 48, 52,
   57, 58, 60, 62, 63, 76, 103, 107, 108,
   125
— shift
    – and assimilation 36
    – process of 53, 54
    – to Arabic 108
    – to Russian 114
— social functions 12
— spread 42, 83, 97
— use 4, 122
Lingua franca 11,,16–18, 20, 22, 26, 39,
   42, 61, 75, 76, 81
— Hausa as 129
— Russian as 113, 115
— sub-national 16, 26
— urban 63, 64
Linguistic
— and cultural affinity 119
— boundaries 7, 66, 127
— convergence 8
— description of unwritten languages
   12
— diversity 5, 11, 16, 61, 118
    – defining 12
— engineering 88
— fragmentation 45, 48, 50, 55, 70
— geography 30
— heterogeneity 59
— islands 47
— nationalism 105
— pluralism
    – divisive effect of 91
    – the Swiss model of 109
— stratigraphy 30
— unification 22, 64, 68, 105
— uniformity 5
— variation 42, 46
Literacy
— acquisition of 86
— foreign language 87
Long distance trade 22, 36
Luso-African communities 53

Mande languages 26, 45, 55
Manding 26, 31, 51, 66, 81
Manding
— dialects
    – Bambara 28, 43
    – Jula 28, 43

– Mandinka 28, 43
– Maninka 28, 43
— gold trade 33
— interpreters 34
— kingdom 56
— language
– of power 37
– spread 26, 30, 35, 36, 38, 39, 48
— territories 66, 68
— linguistic prestige 41
— migration 52
— social organisation 40
— sociocultural identity 40
— state of Gabu 53
Market languages 82
Migrations 59, 60
Minority
— groups 60, 92, 93
— languages 2, 16, 75, 84, 103, 105
Monolingual
— communities 5
— countries 2
— tribal societies 6
Monolingualism 1, 3, 5, 19, 21
Mother tongue 7, 75, 102, 125, 126
— as symbol of social identity 101
— education 17, 79, 81, 87, 96, 114, 127
Multilingual
— communities 62
— countries 120, 132
— empires 6, 30, 107
— federations 8
— situations, urban 17
— urban centres 61
Multilingualism 1–3, 19
— and communication 20
— and social organisation 4
— and social transition 73
— at district level 17
— historical roots of 9
— horizontal versus vertical 9, 19
— transition from 8
Mutual intelligibility 15

Nation building 79, 88, 122, 131, 133
Nation-states 7
National
— identity, role of lingua francas 82
— language issues 7, 16, 17, 75, 88,
   122, 125
— unity 123, 129

Nationality 106, 111
Nationhood 7, 105, 120, 126
— and linguistic unification 18
— linguistically determined 8, 127
Niger–Gambia trade route 38
Nigerian nationalism 96

Official language 2, 8, 21, 78, 86, 110,
   120, 124
— acquisition of 85
— specialised functional roles of 85
— French, English or Portuguese as
   121
Oral tradition 6, 28
Organisation of African Unity 66, 122

Pacification process 58
Pattern of language use, trifocal 20
Pidgins 82, 101
Pluralism 110, 115
— cultural and linguistic 113
Pluralist language policies 126–127
Portuguese
— sources 34, 50, 52, 54
— traders 51
— trading stations 38
Principle of nationalities 112–114
Pulaar 66

Royal bard or jeli 41

Silent barter 34
Slave trade, sociolinguistic conse-
   quences of 56, 57
Slave villages 57, 58
Small stratified societies 51
Social and linguistic fragmentation 48,
   56, 60
Social function of language 100
Sociolinguistic
— behaviour 132
— profile 73, 77
— research, aim of 2
Sociolinguistics 11
Southern Mande languages 51, 68
Special status languages 17, 76
Spread of lingua francas, role of cultu-
   ral factors 84
Standard language 21, 22, 102
Supra-ethnic states 31
Surveys

— of languages and language use 15
— sociolinguistic 130, 131
Swahili 123, 126
Swiss federalism 109
Symbolic function of language 40–42

Territorial principle 109
Trade route, Upper Niger to the Atlan-
    tic coast 52
Trade, Portuguese 46
Trans-Saharan route 31, 56
Transition 3, 7
Tribalism 3, 91, 121
'Trifocal' pattern of language use 86

UNESCO 75, 78, 122
Urban migration 62, 64
Urbanisation 83

Vertical multilingualism 30
Voltaic languages 70

Wave theory 15
West Atlantic languages 45, 55, 70
Wolof 63, 83

Yoruba 94, 127